CAMBRIDGE

CAMBRIDGE

*Historical Text
by Douglas Ferguson*

*The Cambridge Phenomenon
by Nick Segal*

*Photographs
by Dona Haycraft*

Covent Garden Press, Cambridge

First published in the UK by Covent Garden Press, Cambridge, 52 Covent
Garden, Cambridge 1987.

Designed by John Chalmers.
Typeset in 11pt Palatino from disc by Tocatta Graphics Ltd.,
116 Southwark Street, London SE1.
Litho origination by Waterden Reproductions Ltd.,
East Cross Centre, Waterden Road, London E15.
Printed at the Roundwood Press, Kineton, Warwick.
Bound by Dorstel Press Ltd.,
Edinburgh Way, Temple Fields, Harlow, Essex CM20 2DH.

ISBN 0-9512578-0-3

Contents

Preface by the Publishers

We would like to thank the following for the use of material and for allowing us to take particular photographs.

Br. Thomas Anthony SSF, Priest-in-Charge of St Bene't's Church.
The Master and Fellows of St Catharine's College.
The Cavendish Laboratory.
The Master and Fellows of Clare College.
The Vicar of St. Edward's Church.
The Master and Fellows of Emmanuel College.
The Drawing Office, Department of Geography, University of Cambridge.
The Master and Fellows of Jesus College.
The Provost and Fellows of King's College.
The Master and Fellows of Pembroke College.
The Master and Fellows of Peterhouse.
Peter Lofts Studio.
The President and Fellows of Queens' College.
The Master and Fellows of Trinity College.
Photograph of Professor Needham courtesy of Mrs Needham.

We hope that people and colleges not specifically mentioned but whose co-operation is much appreciated, will also accept our thanks.

We would also like to thank the Cambridge University Press for permission to quote from G.M. Trevelyan's book *Trinity College, An Historical Sketch*. Sir Nikolaus Pevsner's *Cambridgeshire* in the *Buildings of England* series and the Survey and Inventory *City of Cambridge* by the Royal Commission on Historical Monuments have been invaluable sources for architectural information. *Cambridge Commemorated* compiled by Laurence and Helen Fowler has provided interesting details on University life.

During the course of production we have received a great deal of encouragement and support from friends. There are people whom we would like to thank for generously giving their time and expertise: Mike Ashby, Sid Busby, Henry Button, Michael Coles, John Deakin, John Drury, Anthony Edwards, Keith Garbett, Neil Hammond, Walter Herriot, Tim Hobbs, Gary Law, Alison Lowe, David McKitterick, Mike Petty, Jim Roseblade, Adam Sisman, Frank Stubbings, David Watkin and Hilary Wayment. Ian Gulley drew the maps against the clock with considerable calm.

This is the first book published by the Covent Garden Press, Cambridge. In a project as wide-ranging as this there are many pitfalls. We hope that anyone finding mistakes will write to us in order that they can be put right in the second edition.

Chapter 1

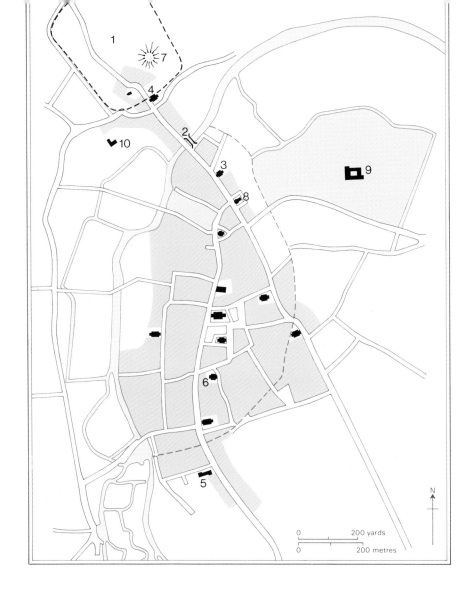

1. Roman settlement
2. Roman ford or bridge
3. St Clement's Church
4. St Giles' Church
5. Little St Mary's Church
6. St Bene't's Church
7. Castle
8. Round Church
9. Benedictine Priory
10. School of Pythagoras

Town sites
Religious sites

St Bene't's tower, the oldest stonework in the city. Corpus Christi, who used the church for over two centuries, made a bridge from its Old Court into the church.

Before the University

Cambridge owes its location and early importance to the river. In the first century A.D. the newly-arrived Romans, as part of a network of communications between their principal garrisons, needed a direct road to link Colchester with Leicester and Chester. One of the many barriers this road had to overcome was the River Cam, and the Romans forded it or may have erected a wooden bridge close to where Magdalene Bridge now stands. A small settlement grew up on the slope of the hill to the north-west, but it was never very important and no trace of it is visible, although remains were uncovered recently when foundations were dug for the extension to Shire Hall. The Roman road, however (allowing for one or two slight deviations), is substantially the same as the present road which cuts through the city and which has several names between Hills Road and Huntingdon Road. It is really the sole legacy of the Romans, though the notion of Roman Cambridge has been useful to establish the antiquity of the town, especially when confronting the Saxon origins of Oxford.

The Saxon tower arch of St Bene't's derived from Continental predecessors. The carvings of primitive animals on the arch mouldings are nearly a thousand years old.

When the Angles and Saxons arrived, around the middle of the fifth century, the river appears to have become a boundary, for when eventually the Dark Ages became less obscure there were two distinct settlements, the larger to the south-east of the river belonging to the East Angles, that to the north-west an outpost of the Mercians. Each had its own field system and market. Towards the end of the ninth century the Danes came and until well into the next century Cambridge was part of the Danelaw. Nothing remains visible, but a church on the important road leading to the river is dedicated to St Clement, a favourite Danish saint. There are references in the Anglo-Saxon Chronicle to Grantaceastr, the Danish army, and in 875 to Grantebryg, the first reference in English to a bridge.

What few remains there are of Saxon Cambridge come from the eleventh century when the town was a flourishing settlement, both parts now united, with bridge, market and several churches. There is an arch built into the Victorian Church of St Giles, some fragments at the western end of Little St Mary's and above all the tower of St Bene't's, the oldest building in Cambridge. This splendid tower has unmistakable long and short work at its corners and in its top stage distinctive twin bell openings separated by a turned baluster. But inside, supporting the arch leading into the nave, are two curious animals whose primitive forms bring us at once into contact with the strange, recently pagan, society which carved them. The chief legacy of Saxons and Danes was the basic shape of the town, protected on one side by the River Cam and on the other by a ditch, which was to be reinforced several times in the next few centuries and named the "King's Ditch". A second major road forked southwards from the former Roman road along the line of the modern Trumpington Street.

The coming of the Normans consolidated the status of the town. A motte and bailey castle (built as a base from which to mount operations against Hereward the Wake in the fen country to the north) confirmed Cambridge as the leading town of the shire, with the headquarters of the Sheriff. Churches were rebuilt and the Round Church erected at the most important road junction. A priory for Augustinian canons was founded near the castle, though it quickly moved to Barnwell, to the east of the town near Newmarket Road, and a small Benedictine nunnery was founded just outside the King's Ditch. The best visible remains of these buildings are few but striking. There is extensive arcading in the north transept of the nunnery church, built with money given by Malcolm IV of Scotland and Earl of Huntingdon and now the chapel of Jesus College. Inside the Round Church are eight great round piers with an assortment of capitals. This is one of five English churches built in a circular form to commemorate the Church of the Holy Sepulchre in Jerusalem, but other apparently Norman features date from a severe restoration in 1841. Well outside the mediaeval town, on the Newmarket road, is the small church of a long-vanished leper hospital. The chancel arch and some windows contain good twelfth century carvings.

By the end of the twelfth century Cambridge was a small but prosperous town, well placed on a navigable river connecting via the Great Ouse with the sea at King's Lynn. Cambridge already had a Mayor, there were wharves along the river, approached by lanes containing merchants' warehouses, and there were large mills and numerous inns. One stone house, the so-called School of Pythagoras (now part of St John's College) survives from this time to bear witness to the wealth of at least some of the trading community. King John gave charters to the town in 1201 and 1207, in which merchants obtained extensive privileges and in 1210 a fair was established on Stourbridge Common, a fair which was to develop into one of the greatest fairs in Europe.

With these advantages Cambridge's position as an important market town seemed assured. The Church maintained a notable presence with a dozen fine parish churches and Barnwell Priory was rapidly growing in importance. Such was the town into which the first scholars came in 1209.

The motte of Cambridge castle from which Norman sheriffs once ruled the county, now surrounded by buildings and dominated by the modern Shire Hall complex.

The Coming of the Clerks

Up to this time learning was centred around the monasteries, which were virtually the only places where facilities existed for study and teaching. Many had built up long-established traditions of scholarship and had acquired large collections of manuscripts. But by the twelfth century more and more scholars were finding that the rigid doctrine of the Church and the traditional teaching of the monastic orders were proving increasingly unsatisfactory. There was very little opportunity to ask questions, let alone challenge accepted beliefs, and in their search for like minds to help them pursue their quest for knowledge scholars tended to congregate in cities such as Bologna, Salerno or Paris. The monasteries were in fact being replaced as places of learning by what were later to be called universities, though the change would not be completed for several centuries.

Paris was particularly popular with English students, and when in 1169 Henry II recalled them from Paris the obvious substitute in England was Oxford, with its royal palace and two large monasteries, and where there was a growing number of teachers and scholars. The later years of the twelfth century saw a dramatic growth in numbers, with organisation into faculties containing Doctors and Masters and a structure of disciplines.

In 1209 a more than usually serious disturbance at Oxford led to a large number fleeing in fear of their lives. A student at archery practice accidentally killed a townswoman and this provoked a swift reaction resulting in several scholars being summarily hanged. How or why the fugitives reached Cambridge is not clear. There is no record of scholars in the town before then, but there may have been some kind of monastic schools. In any case, as a prosperous town with good communications with eastern England, London and the north, Cambridge would have been an attractive place to stay.

After 1209 numbers seem to have grown rapidly and within twenty years or so there was already some organisation of Masters (the teachers) with an elected Chancellor at their head. Teachers and students all lived in lodgings in the town, and lectures took place wherever suitable places could be found. Soon houses were hired as hostels for students, with a Master in charge (in 1280 there were already thirty-four such hostels), and this was to be how students were accommodated for at least two hundred years. Usually about fourteen or fifteen years old, they were badly disciplined and often caused disturbances; on the other hand Cambridge citizens not infrequently overcharged for rooms and food. From the beginning the influx of large numbers of strangers meant the likelihood of friction or worse.

Two late Norman windows from the chapel of the former leper hospital near Barnwell outside the town. Given by the University to the Cambridgeshire Preservation Society who restored it.

Twelfth century merchant's house, long known as the "School of Pythagoras" from the fanciful notion that Pythagoras once taught there. Now used by students of St John's.

With the encouragement of the Church and the ultimate backing of the King the University began to grow more powerful. It acquired privileges and certain controls over the town, including joint supervision of markets, rents, food prices and recreation. Masters and scholars had the right to trial by Chancellor's court, where punishments were much less severe than in civil courts. After riots in the town, for instance, scholars usually escaped with fines whereas the townsmen's ringleaders could be hanged. In such circumstances the town's self-confidence was undermined, and it is ironic that just as Cambridge was settling down to a growing degree of self-government, independent of the Sheriff, it should find itself subject to irksome interference by the University, a state of affairs which was to last well into the nineteenth century. The town's Mayor and Bailiffs had to swear an oath to maintain the privileges of the University, while the Chancellor had the power to punish any offences against scholars. He could, for example, imprison in the castle any layman guilty of assaulting a scholar. It was hardly surprising that there was constantly recurring ill-feeling between town and gown, or that it should occasionally break out in violence. The town could do very little without the consent of the University.

During the thirteenth century all the principal orders of friars arrived in Cambridge, a further indication of the town's importance. Friars, unlike monks, went out into the world as preachers, and as their orders contained many learned men they were to play a major part in the teaching of the University until the dissolution, especially the Dominicans, the Franciscans and the Austin Friars.

In 1284 (after an unsuccessful attempt four years earlier) came the founding of the first college, Peterhouse. Others followed and in 1318 Cambridge was declared by the Pope a *studium generale*, or university, with its graduates licensed to teach anywhere in Christendom.

University and Colleges

It is important to understand the difference between University and colleges and their relationship with each other. Both terms originally meant groups of people, rather than the buildings they used: a university (Latin, *universitas*) was the whole body of teachers and scholars, a college (Latin, *collegium*) a number living together and engaged in a common pursuit, in this case learning. The University began with no buildings of its own, with teachers and students all living wherever they could find accommodation, and with lectures and classes held in any large enough place. Gradually authority was imposed by the body of Masters acting collectively to control teaching and discipline.

The functioning of the University derives from its statutes, which have the authority of the Queen in Council and of Parliament and which have been altered and amended over the centuries. The head of the University is the Chancellor, often an eminent figure from public life (at present HRH Prince Philip, the Duke of Edinburgh), elected by the Senate for life, but he is not always present in Cambridge and a Vice-Chancellor is elected for two years from the heads of colleges to preside over the running of the University. A recent exception to this was Lord Adrian, Master of Clare College, who was first Vice-Chancellor and then Chancellor. On the whole Cambridge University has been well served by its Chancellors. John Fisher and Lord Burghley in the sixteenth century and Prince Albert in the nineteenth were all instrumental in bringing about much-needed changes which improved the standing and the working of the University. Most of the others had the wisdom to carry out their duties with dignity, without attempting to interfere in its internal affairs. The prominence of the Chancellor's position has not, in the past, made for security; seven have ended their period of office on the executioner's block.

The legislative authority is Regent House, made up of teaching Masters of Arts, professors and some administrators, and this votes on proposals (or Graces, from Latin, *gratia*; Latin was the official language of the University until the nineteenth century and is still used in certain official acts and ceremonies). It also elects a smaller Council of the Senate, the principal administrative authority. Through these bodies and with the help of the Financial Board, the General Board of the Faculties and the various Faculty Boards, the University oversees what is taught, arranges

syllabuses and lectures, appoints professors and lecturers and confers degrees. The Senate, to which all Masters of Arts belong whether resident or not, has the right to discuss and to propose amendments, but it now meets only to elect the Chancellor or to vote on certain Graces of particular importance. Two Proctors are appointed as the University's disciplinary officers. Their importance has declined since the Middle Ages and they no longer patrol the streets at night with their posse of constables ("bulldogs"), but they still check examination rooms and have duties at Council meetings (Congregations) and at degree ceremonies.

The University now possesses some administrative buildings together with many lecture rooms, laboratories and faculty buildings with their libraries. It also supervises the University Library, the University Press, the Botanic Garden and the Fitzwilliam Museum. It is financed partly by the government, through the University Grants Committee, and partly by the colleges.

Individual students, however, do not belong directly to the University, but to one of the colleges. The University is really a federation of the colleges, at present thirty-one in number. Of these, twenty-five are colleges with undergraduates (though with a proportion of post-graduates) and six are graduate colleges (two of which also admit some undergraduates). Originally all were for men only, until two were founded for women in the late nineteenth century followed by a third for women in 1954. Since 1972, however, a gradual change has seen all except two of the women's colleges accepting both sexes.

From 1284 onwards colleges were founded one by one to provide places for living and studying for small numbers of Fellows (from Latin *socius*, a companion). The founder was usually a wealthy man or woman from the court, from a noble family or from the Church, and he or she would buy a site, give money to erect buildings and endow the college with land to produce income for its survival. The act of foundation was often done with the aim of producing more clergy or administrators for the nation, but in the Middle Ages it was also a religious act linked with the provision of masses to be said for the founder's soul.

Each college is an independent body with its own statutes, owning its own land and buildings (and responsible for their upkeep), electing its own Fellows and admitting its own students. Its governing body consists of all or some of its Fellows and has at its head a Master (sometimes called a Provost, President or Principal). The original endowment, augmented by subsequent benefactions and investments, provides income to maintain a varying number of Fellows, who act as tutors, lecturers and administrators. These senior members are sometimes called "dons", from Latin *dominus*. When Trinity College was founded in 1546 from the amalgamation of King's Hall and Michaelhouse, their incomes were taken over and vastly increased (mostly from estates confiscated from dissolved religious houses). Trinity's annual income in the mid-sixteenth

Private study in the Sherlock Library, St Catharine's College. Part of the working day of Cambridge students for eight centuries.

century has been estimated at £1,600, a very large sum at that time. Since then the value of Trinity's estates has increased through careful management and more land has been bought. Income from land has always been an essential factor in a college's prosperity. Even small colleges have an important business side managed by the college Bursar.

By the fifteenth century junior students too began to reside in the colleges. They were known as "pensioners" because they paid for their accommodation, or "undergraduates" because they were supervised by graduates. Each college provides rooms for meals, accommodation, recreation and facilities for private study. It is, in effect, a hall of residence, though because of the individual tuition given there, and the presence of distinguished scholars, it is much more than that.

All the colleges have maintained a tradition of not specialising in a particular subject and thus it is possible to study most subjects in each college. Some colleges have built up a reputation in certain subjects, as Trinity Hall has for law or Downing for medicine. Cambridge follows a distinctive method of tuition, which is arranged partly by the colleges and partly by the University. The latter organises lectures, seminars and laboratory work in University buildings and these are attended by students from all colleges. The college assigns each student to a Director of Studies, whose task it is to arrange the student's programme of work by means of supervisions; the student works individually with a supervisor (who is not necessarily of the same college) in a college or faculty room or in the supervisor's own house. The work is personal and intensive, and each student has a room for private work and access to several libraries, in his college and faculty besides the University Library.

During the Middle Ages a pattern of building based on the experience of monastic houses emerged to cover the basic needs of a college. For safety the buildings faced inwards round a courtyard, with a strong gate as in castles, fortified houses and farms. The most important was the hall, a large room for meals and assemblies. The head of the college, the Master, had a separate apartment, like the abbot or prior, as he too had to entertain guests from time to time. From the fourteenth century colleges began to build their own chapels because nearly all the scholars were in holy orders and daily services were an essential part of college life. Other rooms were for the Fellows, with later a room for the growing number of books and accommodation for undergraduates. With great monasteries like Ely and Barnwell close at hand there was no shortage of masons and carpenters to carry out skilled work, while it is possible that some of the unskilled work was carried out by scholars themselves.

The story of the Cambridge colleges is that of the gradual enrichment and growth of these constituent parts. They still form the nucleus of the modern college. Later additions have been mainly to provide further room for increasing numbers. Because for most of their history the colleges have been at least comfortably off, they have been able to employ good architects, craftsmen and materials. Those colleges founded in the Middle Ages contained only a handful of men. Today their numbers have risen to several hundreds, and in addition they employ a great many porters, kitchen and dining room staff, office workers, librarians, gardeners, maintenance men and others. Each is a busy community, which has built up its own traditions and character over the years.

An earlier scholar, from a rare English illuminated copy of the Romance of Alexander, mid-thirteenth century. The text is in Anglo-Norman, the everyday language of most early Cambridge students.

Chapter 2

1. Hospital of St John
2. Old Court, Peterhouse
3. Castle
4. King's Hall
5. Michaelhouse
6. Clare Hall
7. Pembroke College
8. Gonville College
9. Trinity Hall
10. Corpus Christi College
11. Old Schools Court
12. Buckingham College
13. King's College Chapel
14. St Catharine's College
15. Queens' College
16. Great St Mary's Church

Town sites
Religious sites
University sites

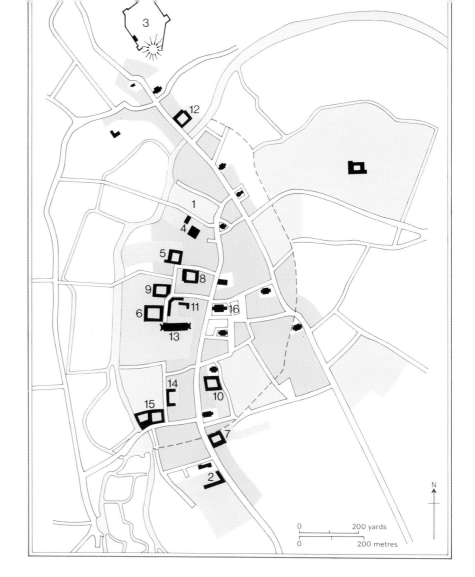

The ancient and modern heart of the city, ecclesiastical and commercial, town and gown; Great St Mary's towers over the stalls on Market Hill.

Early Years

Scholars discovered that ordinary lodgings were unsatisfactory and many chose to live in hostels, which had some sort of communal life. Some of these were fairly large, even sometimes with a small chapel, but they had no endowment and so their existence must have been precarious. There is a long list of hostels closing and others being started. In 1280, however, Hugh de Balsham, Bishop of Ely, took the first step towards a place of residence for scholars by accommodating a small number in part of the already existing Hospital of St John, a refuge for the elderly and infirm situated where St John's College is now.

The arrangement was not happy and the Bishop in 1284 moved his scholars into two houses in Trumpington Street, just outside the town gate. Hugh de Balsham was in fact doing much the same as a fellow bishop, Walter de Merton, had already done at Oxford. Both were encouraging learning in the two towns, and both made it clear that their foundations were to be non-monastic. It is interesting, but tantalising, to

The crowded mediaeval town. Peterhouse's hall, with lantern, stair turret and Tudor chimneys rising above a sea of town roofs across Trumpington Street.

recall that Merton College could have been founded in Cambridge, for the Bishop had bought land in both places. On Hugh's death two years later a bequest came to the scholars and they built their first communal building, a hall close behind their two houses. The two original hostels were pulled down long ago and the hall is much altered. Nevertheless, the old court has seen succeeding generations of scholars for over seven hundred years. As their chapel they used St Peter's Church immediately to the north, from which the College took its name. Soon it was able to buy further land to the south and within sixty years of its foundation Peterhouse received statutes (based on those of Merton College) making provision for a Master and fourteen Fellows. At about the same time the Church was rebuilt and rededicated to St Mary. Such a beginning is typical of most of the early Cambridge colleges. Life would have been simple, and accommodation and food far from luxurious, but scholars would have been able to settle down to their studies with some sense of security.

While Peterhouse was building its hall, Edward I was in Cambridge making additions to the castle. Round the Norman motte with its wooden palisade arose a stone curtain wall, with several towers and a great gate, with a hall and lodgings contained inside its circuit. Though Cambridge Castle was not as large as the castles Edward built in North Wales, it was meant to impress on all the power of the King. This was the castle's one period of splendour, and Edward I was the only king to stay in it, for not much more than a century later materials were being carted away for college building and not a stone remains visible now. The Great Gate was the last to go, in 1842. National defences were relatively as expensive and as short-lived then as now.

The successful launching of Peterhouse encouraged further foundations, and in the first half of the fourteenth century King's Hall, Michaelhouse, Clare, Pembroke, Gonville, Trinity Hall and Corpus Christi came into existence between 1317 and 1352 (the first two were merged two centuries later into Trinity College). Several of them were built on land near the river where there had been quays and merchants' houses, which suggests that there was some decline in river trade at the time. Perhaps the developing University was acting as a brake on the town's fortunes or perhaps commerce was concentrating in other parts of the town. For whatever reason we should be thankful, for in this way originated one of the most beautiful and distinctive features of Cambridge, "the Backs", where college buildings and houses make such a harmonious composition with the Cam.

The water-meadows of Coe Fen and Laundress Green with King's Chapel and Queens' College in the background show the Backs as they have been for centuries.

Founding a college had come to be seen as a religious act comparable with the founding of a monastery or the enrichment of a church. Corpus Christi was founded, uniquely, by the town guilds largely with the aim of having prayers said for departed guild members. But there was also both a genuine desire and an urgent need for more numerous and better educated clergy, as well as for more administrators, lawyers and physicians in a society which was gradually becoming more sophisticated. After a third of England's population had died in the Black Death of 1348-9 the need became really acute.

The buildings of these early colleges were utilitarian rather than grand. This is shown not only in their small scale, but also in the materials used for their construction. They were built of rubble, irregular pieces of stone, or a soft local stone called clunch, which weathers badly. As Cambridge has no natural deposits of good stone, all needed for college, church or castle had to be brought from Stamford or Rutland, by a network of rivers. It was expensive, and so good quality stone was used sparingly for dressings.

Quite soon the advantages of a closed court were realised, with ranges of buildings on four sides, creating a sense of privacy and the tranquillity necessary for study, as well as safety in case of disturbances in the town. There are two places where some idea of such a court can be appreciated today. In Trinity Hall, even though the interior of the court was refaced with dressed stone in the eighteenth century and one range has been rebuilt completely, there is a feeling of intimacy. At the back of the north range, out of sight of eighteenth century visitors, the original rubble and clunch can be plainly seen, patched here and there with brick, and with some original fourteenth century windows still visible.

It is the Old Court of Corpus Christi, intact save for one corner, which gives the best idea of a fourteenth century college. It has two storeys with hall and adjacent Master's lodge, and a number of original windows. The rooms appear to have been arranged in sets, with one larger common room for sleeping and up to four cubicles for study. The buttresses, plaster and attic rooms came later. There was no chapel, since the neighbouring Parish Church of St Bene't was used for worship. Indeed most of these early colleges used local churches and continued to do so even though, like Trinity Hall, a chapel was included in the court. Pembroke was the first college to use its own chapel, licensed by the Pope in 1355, and built as part of the court, once one of the smallest of all courts. But this chapel is not now used as such, and demolitions and alterations make it hard to visualise Pembroke's court as it once was. Behind later ashlar, however, the street facade still gives an idea of the original, with two gables and the only surviving fourteenth century college gate in between.

One more building should be noted, the first erected by the University itself, a lecture room for the highest branch of learning, Divinity. The course of studies pursued at Cambridge was that common to universities

The entrance gate of Pembroke College survives from the fourteenth century. The surrounding walls were refaced four hundred years later.

The Old Court of Corpus Christi, the oldest court of any Cambridge college. The Cavendish Laboratory, where Thompson discovered the electron and Rutherford split the atom, appears above the roof.

all over Europe and it was divided into two parts, the Trivium of three years and the Quadrivium of four. The Trivium, consisting of Grammar, Logic and Rhetoric, gave grounding in Latin syntax, correct thinking and how to use language effectively. The Quadrivium changed the emphasis to a study of nature and consisted of Music (theoretical not practical), Arithmetic, Geometry and Astronomy. Parallel with both parts the Three Philosophies (Moral, Metaphysical and Natural) and the two Learned Tongues, Greek and Hebrew, were studied. Lectures, disputations and examinations were in Latin. There was much hard work involved, Roman, rather than Arabic numerals were used and, before the invention of printing, manuscripts were wearisomely copied.

At the end of seven years a successful student became a Master of Arts, which gave him a licence to teach and in effect assured his future. In modern times the tradition continues, though a degree course now normally takes three years and the Master of Arts degree is conferred as a formality six years from the end of the student's first term. Some students studied one of the higher faculties, Law (Canon or Civil), Medicine or Theology. Such students would be aiming at a position in the King's service or the higher ranks of the Church.

The Divinity School, built during the second half of the fourteenth century, was the start of a plan to provide rooms for lectures and disputations. It is a two-storey building, of rubble, with a meeting room above the lecture room for Regent (or teaching) Masters, and it forms one range of a four-sided cobbled court. Although the other ranges are later, and one was completely re-built in the eighteenth century, the Old Schools Court is one of the most evocative corners of Cambridge. It has been the heart of the University, the resort of its finest scholars, for six centuries.

In these buildings, the two or three college courts and the Divinity School, it is not difficult to recall the early University. They are impressive for their antiquity, for the memories they evoke of the scholars who taught or listened there. But there was as yet no fine architecture in Cambridge as there already was in Oxford. The lovely tower of Merton Chapel and the soaring spire of St Mary's Church are signs of a different world. Above all William of Wykeham's New College, beautifully planned and executed, was a portent of splendours to come.

More important in Cambridge were the churches, reflecting the authority the Bishop of Ely had over town and University. St Michael and St Mary the Less (which as St Peter had given its name to Peterhouse) were both re-built at around the same time as the two masterpieces of mediaeval art at Ely, the cathedral's Lady Chapel and the Octagon, both the inspiration of the sacrist Alan of Walsingham. It is not fanciful to suppose that the flowing decorated tracery in the windows of these churches owes much to the mother cathedral only sixteen miles away.

To a citizen of Cambridge the dominance of the Church must have been overwhelming. In addition to parish churches and their clergy, about a third of the town belonged to religious houses of the monasteries and the four major orders of friars. Now the colleges, whose members were all in holy orders, were growing more numerous and confident. Small wonder, that when in 1381 the Peasants Revolt spread to Cambridge, the townspeople rose against the much resented scholars. The University Chest in Great St Mary's Church was broken open and plundered, deeds and records were destroyed and the Chancellor was compelled to sign a document giving up the University's rights over the town. They were of course quickly recovered when order was restored, leaving bitter feelings on both sides. Seven years later Richard II held Parliament in Cambridge, lodging with his court in Barnwell Priory, and the positions of Chancellor and University were strengthened.

We can gain some impression of the buildings of the unpretentious fourteenth century University town, but what of the people who lived and studied there? For the most part they are shadowy figures, but if we turn to a contemporary author we can build up some sort of picture. Chaucer's inn-keeper, merchant, guildsman, even Wife of Bath could be townspeople of Cambridge, the prioress, monk, friar and parish priest

The wild garden in the graveyard of Little St Mary's, formerly St Peter's, the church once used by Peterhouse, overlooked by seventeenth century town houses.

recognisable figures of the Church. Chaucer set the Reeve's Tale in Trumpington, so he may have visited Cambridge. The quiet underfed clerk must have been typical of many earnest students eager to learn, strong in ideals and quite prepared to put up with a meagre diet and cold rooms in the cause of learning.

A doorway in Magdalene College, with the arms of Walden Abbey: a reminder of the Benedictine monks who lived and studied there before the Dissolution of the Monasteries.

Mediaeval Growth

In the latter part of the mid-fourteenth century the resources of England were used to carry on the Hundred Years War with France. There was also a change of dynasty, with Henry IV deposing Richard II to seize power for the House of Lancaster, and this led to a period of unrest in which the new King contended with his rebellious nobles. With the King's attention thus diverted, and with much money required to pay for these wars, the universities had to continue as best they could. Their existence was not in doubt as trained men were still needed to help Church and State, but it was certainly not a time for expansion.

On the other hand, the universities had a chance to settle down, and when expansion came it was to be in a more substantial form. In Cambridge, the first sign of this was at King's Hall, founded a century earlier on a small scale by Edward II and enlarged by his son Edward III. Like the rest of the early colleges its buildings were not spectacular, but in 1428-32 it acquired a new gatehouse in King's Childers Lane (named after the boys provided for by the King's foundation and which has long since vanished). King Edward's Tower was the first of the splendid series of Cambridge college gatehouses, all of them tall, with octagonal turrets at their corners. It is no longer quite in its original form (or indeed in its original place), but it remains nevertheless Cambridge's first college building on a grand scale. The statue of Edward III, after whom the tower is named, is Elizabethan.

About the same time as the tower was originally built, Benedictine monks from four great abbeys (Croyland, Ely, Ramsey and Walden) combined to build a college for their order. Small numbers of monks had taken part in university studies for some time, but this new college was a sign that monasteries had come to recognise that the most influential teachers and scholars were now to be found, not in their own houses but in the universities. The college was called Buckingham College after the powerful Duke who was a great benefactor. It was suppressed at the Dissolution of the Monasteries and was later refounded as Magdalene College. Its early days are still recalled in the Monk's Room in the First Court and by the arms of the four monasteries over some of the doorways.

Then, quite suddenly, came the founding of King's College by Henry VI. This college too was fated to carry on its existence in small cramped quarters for not far short of four centuries and the great chapel took nearly a hundred years to complete. But the provision of the King for no less than seventy Fellows, with priests, clerks and choristers in addition, and the size of the chapel (revealed soon by its foundations), as well as the large area of land enclosed in the heart of the town, all showed the unprecedented size of the new college.

As if the country had not endured enough, it now had to contend with civil wars, the Wars of the Roses. Later generations may look back on

Henry VI as "the royal saint" of Wordsworth's sonnet, but in his own day his weak, incompetent rule was a sure recipe for insurrection. For Cambridge this was a time of poverty and decline and recurring plagues in a town made more crowded by the expansion of the University. There was some enlargement of parish churches but that was because of the need to provide for more side altars, rather than a rising population. One church, St Edward's, acquired its large side aisles for the use of Trinity Hall and Clare Hall, which had previously used the Church of St John Zachary, demolished to make way for King's College.

In the second half of the fifteenth century the University grew still more through two colleges which owe their existence to King's, through further lecture rooms and by taking the lead in the rebuilding of the church which had become the University Church.

One of the colleges was the small Catharine Hall (now St Catharine's), the only college to be founded by the current head of another, Robert Woodlarke, Provost of King's. The other was Queens', where Henry VI's Queen, Margaret of Anjou, took an interest in a small college, St Bernard, which had been founded by the Rector of St Botolph's, Andrew Dokett. Dokett had bequeathed the site of a hostel to the College when it was granted a charter by Henry VI in 1447. Although only eighteen years old, Queen Margaret was strong-willed and intelligent, and encouraged by the powerful Cardinal Beaufort (an early benefactor of the College) she petitioned the King to be allowed to found the College "to laud and honneure of sexe feminine", perhaps to emulate her husband who was then founding King's College. In 1448 Henry VI enabled the Queen to refound the College under the name of Queen's College of St Margaret and St Bernard.

The Old Court at Queens' was completed in under two years, probably under the direction of a local master mason Reginald Ely, who was engaged also on the first phase of building at King's College. Reginald Ely chose brick, a relatively cheap material which had already been used in Henry VI's other foundation, Eton College near Windsor. Old Court remains the best example of a complete mediaeval enclosed court, incorporating chapel, hall, kitchen, library, gate tower and living rooms. The use of red brick with stone dressings for windows, doorways and the corners of towers make a particularly picturesque combination.

Around 1460 the College was extended, again probably by Reginald Ely, to provide extra accommodation. A cloister walk was made as part of the plan of the new court, the first such cloister in Cambridge. Cloisters were of course common in monasteries and cathedrals and there was already one at New College, Oxford. Their general absence in Cambridge colleges is perhaps because they were not considered necessary. Money could be better spent on more important things.

Shortly afterwards Edward IV's Queen Elizabeth Woodville (who had been one of Queen Margaret's Ladies-in-Waiting) took the College

The cloisters of Queens' College.

under her protection and later gave it its statutes in which she is referred to as "true foundress by right of succession". The position of the apostrophe in Queens' recognises this double royal patronage.

It is sad to record the later stories of the two royal ladies: Margaret's son was brutally killed at the battle of Tewkesbury, while Elizabeth's two sons were the princes murdered in the Tower of London. However, Andrew Dokett continued as the first President of Queens' for over thirty-five years into the reign of Richard III. For a short period the College was to be wealthy when Richard III endowed it with "great rents" but unfortunately these belonged to lands he had confiscated. When Richard came to grief at Bosworth Field, Henry VII restored them to their original owners.

The University's own additions were nothing like as well made or beautiful. Between the 1430's and 1470's three more ranges were added to the Divinity School; two of them of brick, by then a respectable material. They now made a small enclosed court, the only buildings owned by the University until the eighteenth century. The Old Schools have since been altered several times, and the east range completely rebuilt.

Since the earliest days of the University the Church of St Mary the Great had been much used as a place of worship, meetings of the Regent Masters, disputations and University ceremonies. The University Chest containing records and documents was kept in the Church. Now, with the importance of the University growing steadily, the Church was too small and not sufficiently grand. To meet the cost of rebuilding it in a more worthy manner, University officials travelled throughout the Kingdom seeking donations. Kings, noblemen, bishops, abbots and priors, with more humble people, contributed through gifts of money or timber. The titles and arms of many of them are recorded in the nineteenth century glass in the nave windows.

Building began in 1478 and went on for forty years. The style is Late Perpendicular in which many East Anglian churches were built, churches such as Saffron Walden, Long Melford, Lavenham and, nearer home, Burwell. They are embattled on the outside, with large windows and tall towers. Inside tall slender shafts support lofty arches, and there is much fine carving in the spandrels and in the panels between the windows. In this latest form Great St Mary's was indeed a fitting church for an increasingly influential University.

So the end of the fifteenth century and the start of the sixteenth saw building in progress on two fine buildings, in their day the two most splendid in the town. Great St Mary proceeded steadily, with the chancel in use after a few years. King's College Chapel across the road took longer and its story needs elaboration.

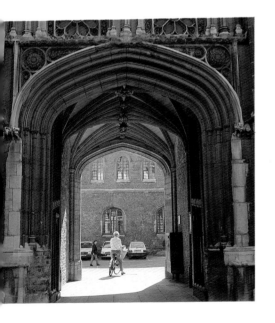

The ancient gateway to King's College, now the way to the University offices in Old Schools for University messengers on their bicycles.

*"Where the bright Seraphim in burning row
Their loud up-lifted Angel trumpets blow,
And the Cherubick host in thousand quires
Touch their immortal Harps of golden wires"
- Milton.*

King's College Chapel

King Henry VI was a studious, devout man who had grown up in a country disillusioned by the disastrous conclusion of the French wars. In 1441, when he was 21 years old and had already founded a school for boys at Eton, he made plans for a small college in Cambridge with a Rector and twelve Fellows, on a cramped site just behind the Divinity School.

What prompted the King to enlarge his college only two years later is not certain. His declared aim was "to extirpate heresies, to increase the number of clergy and to provide ministers of religion whose life and doctrine would give light to his subjects", and the enlarged college should therefore be seen not merely as an expression of the King's faith but also as a bastion against heresy, such as that of the Lollards and Wyclif. Had Oxford not then been so much involved with Wyclif's ideas on Church reform Henry would very likely have chosen to build his College there, as it was closer to Eton. But he hated the unorthodox, and Cambridge gained a priceless treasure.

Three commissioners were sent to Cambridge to obtain sufficient land to build a college far greater than existed in either university. The site chosen stretched from the main street to the river and involved the destruction of a considerable number of townspeoples' houses and gardens, a small hostel for grammar students, God's House (later to be re-founded as Christ's College) and the Parish Church of St John Zachary. It lay astride an important road leading to the town mills, and a section of this road was therefore closed.

The King's College of the Blessed Mary and St Nicholas was now to have a Provost and no fewer than seventy Fellows, as well as sixteen boy choristers and the same number of chaplains and clerks. His college was planned as a splendid whole, to be built around the sides of a court into which four of the earlier colleges would have fitted comfortably. Henry had a model before him, New College which William of Wykeham, Bishop of Winchester and Chancellor of England, had designed in Oxford towards the end of the fourteenth century. This too had been linked with a boys' school, Winchester College, and was built round a quadrangle containing hall, chapel and Master's Lodge and entered by a monumental gate-tower, the first college built as an integrated whole.

Henry's Will of 1448 states clearly what he intended, and the Chapel, the only part he actually built, shows what a glorious conception it was. Even now the Chapel towers over the city: when it was new it must have soared even higher above houses, colleges and churches, an object of wonder and reverence for scholar and layman. They could have seen comparable splendour only in our cathedrals and abbeys. It is one of the great buildings of Europe, in its fineness of execution, and the way it combines sophisticated engineering with breathtaking beauty.

*"The entrance to a beehive" –
Virginia Woolf.*

Henry's Will reveals that the Chapel's dimensions are much as he planned them. A stone was laid at the high altar by Henry himself on St James's Day, July 25, 1446. The construction took nearly seventy years and the internal fittings another twenty three. The vicissitudes of the Wars of the Roses and the attending scarcity of money confined building to less than thirty of those years spread over three phases. The work of the first fifteen years can be easily seen as the stone used was a Yorkshire limestone, white in colour compared with the creamy Northamptonshire stone used later. All the foundations were laid and some building carried out at the east end, with two side chapels completed. The master mason in charge at this stage was Reginald Ely. There followed a sixteen years break before, in the years 1477-84, the Yorkist kings financed a little more work in the same style. The Chapel had to wait until the first Tudor king, Henry VII, had consolidated the country's finances; then in a final burst of building the main fabric was finished between 1508 and 1515. The number of people employed on the building of the Chapel varied from fifty to over two hundred – a considerable work force for the time when the total population of the town was probably around five thousand.

The Chapel gives the feeling of being built as an inspired unity, even though two distinct styles are apparent. Outside, the change is seen in the buttresses, as the four most westerly ones are much more ornate. Inside the east end – the Chapel proper – the stone-work is as King Henry VI intended the whole Chapel should be, plain and without too much detail or over-elaboration. Reginald Ely, the master mason during this first phase, was responsible for its dignified beauty. The severity of the walls is offset by carvings of angels in groups of four just below the level of the

King Henry VI in his Chapel, part of Provost Robert Hacumblen's brass lectern, given by him in the early sixteenth century.

The doorway of the oldest side chapel; the ogee arch bears the arms of England and the two royal saints, St Edward the Confessor and St Edmund, King of the East Angles.

windows, with more angels as corbels for alternate shafts to the roof and decoration on the ogee arches leading to the most easterly side chapels, all beautifully carved but comparatively small.

To pass from the Chapel to the Antechapel is to enter a different world. The Tudor kings had established a secure dynasty after the uncertainties of the Civil Wars, but felt obliged to boost their somewhat shaky title to the throne by a lavish display of Tudor emblems. The Chapel may be a hymn in stone to the glory of God: the Antechapel is quite definitely a fanfare to the glory of the Tudors. Rose, crown, portcullis, fleur-de-lys, dragon and greyhound, all are everywhere, carved in astonishing detail in each bay by the master carver, Thomas Stockton.

Under the supervision of the master mason for the final phase, John Wastell, came the climax to the work, the fan-vaulted roof. It is arguably the most beautiful ever constructed in stone anywhere, very English in its well ordered, restrained intricacies. The great bosses carved from single blocks of stone, six feet across, and alternating roses with portcullises, alone convey the Tudor message. It is all the more astonishing that, on the evidence of the shafts, the roof vault was not originally planned as fan vaulting.

The Chapel also has stained glass and carved wood of the very highest order, and it is this combination of excellence in a variety of materials that gives it its special greatness. It is difficult to realise that the stained glass and the stone tracery belong to different centuries. The glass is Flemish in style and King Henry VII's glaziers were at work on the twenty-four side windows and the great east window for thirty years after 1515.

One hundred years later: Tudor and Beaufort pageantry, but a monument to the master mason Thomas Stockton too.

From the start the glass followed a master design, depicting "the old law and the new law". Two pictures in the lower parts of each of the side windows tell the story of the Virgin Mary, the life of Christ and the Acts

Opposite, most beautiful of vaulting, John Wastell's masterpiece. The model in the Chapel exhibition, right, shows how the vaulting was constructed and the timber roof above it.

of the Apostles in a sequence which reaches its climax in the east window above the high altar where the Passion and Crucifixion of Christ is depicted in six scenes. In this window the central figure in the upper part is Christ on the Cross, taking upon Himself the burden of the sins of mankind, rising in triumph over the central figure in the lower part, Pontius Pilate, who is washing his hands of his rightful responsibility. Each of the six pictures is crowded with people painted with great subtlety, and the whole is alive with movement and colour.

In the upper part of the side windows scenes from the Old Testament are chosen to make a comment on those from the New Testament below, so we see Jonah cast up by the whale making a parallel with Christ's Resurrection, and the manna falling in the wilderness foreshadowing the Last Supper. The Chapel's glass is the finest and most complete collection of sixteenth century glass anywhere. Even here the Tudors cannot

The window showing the
Betrayal: Judas kisses Christ and
the soldiers move in. St Peter is
about to strike the ear off one of
them.

remain aloof, for in the tracery at the top of each window are over two hundred of their emblems. In particular the red dragon can be seen immediately above the head of Christ on the Cross.

Before the glass was finished work began on the oak screen and stalls. Here the craftsmen were either Italian or French, and the influence is clearly that of the Renaissance. There are friezes and pendants; carved figures, roundels and reliefs abound and so does the King's monogram, HR, interspersed with that of his then Queen, Anne Boleyn.

But it is the way in which each of these masterpieces – sculpture in stone and wood, pictures in glass – combine so easily inside the soaring framework of the Chapel that makes such a tremendous impact. A great painting in a distinctly alien style, the Adoration of the Magi by Rubens, was recently placed in the east end and aroused considerable controversy. Yet now it too has become an integral part of the whole.

The cloisters and the bell tower which Henry VI planned remained unbuilt. College life went on at King's in a court too small for comfort, but the Chapel was an inspiration to the University.

Carved oak stalls, with their canopies and rails. Candles are still used during services.

Chapter 3

Town sites
Religious sites
University sites

Autumn on the Backs.

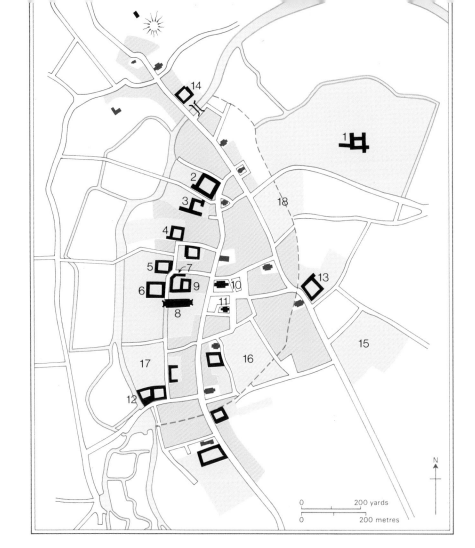

John Fisher

The University was now not merely firmly established but about to play a more important role in the nation's affairs. With the ending of the Wars of the Roses, England was at a turning point and desperately needed peace and a firm ruler to enable her to restore the economy. Under Henry VII England settled down to a period of prosperity and the ideas of the Renaissance could begin to take root.

There were changes in Cambridge too. Numbers were rising and the colleges were more secure financially. Several were now taking pensioners in addition to their Fellows, and teaching in the University was beginning to incorporate something of the New Learning. In effect that meant that some Greek was taught and there was a little more freedom to discuss and challenge traditional doctrines but, most important, a climate was being created in which change was possible.

One significant instance came in 1496 when John Alcock, Bishop of Ely, closed down the once-prosperous Benedictine Priory of St Radegund, just outside the town. The only two remaining nuns were placed

elsewhere and the nunnery buildings converted into a college. Alcock realised that the monasteries no longer had the important function they once had and more colleges were needed in the expanding University. Alcock was Comptroller of the Royal Buildings and a highly competent architect. At Ely he built an ornate chantry chapel for himself in the cathedral and rebuilt the Bishop's Palace and in Cambridge the credit for the rebuilt Great St Mary's is largely his.

At Jesus College (more properly the College of the Blessed Mary the Virgin, St John the Evangelist and the Glorious Virgin St Radegund, but known, as was apparently Alcock's intention, as Jesus College), Alcock could take over a number of monastic buildings with comparatively little alteration, but as the nuns' church was too large, over half the nave was converted into the Master's Lodge and the side aisles shut off; the chancel much enriched became the College Chapel.

So Jesus, founded nearly three hundred years after scholars first came to Cambridge, has older buildings than any other college, built partly before the University was dreamed of. This can be seen in the Norman columns of the nave and especially in the lovely arcading of the Norman north transept. It also continues to benefit from the large grounds of the former Priory, which have provided enough space for subsequent buildings as well as extensive gardens and playing fields. Alcock built a gatehouse in the same style as that at Queens', of patterned brick with a parapet. Like most other parts of the College the gatehouse is liberally adorned with Alcock's punning emblem, the cock perched on an orb. If his intention was to ensure that the Founder's name was not forgotten he can have hit on no better way.

Cambridge was even more fortunate in the man chosen to be Chancellor in 1504. John Fisher was, like Alcock, a Yorkshireman from Beverley and had been Master of Michaelhouse for some years. His reputation as a scholar, his integrity and his clear direction had already marked him out as the outstanding figure in the University. He remained Chancellor for over thirty years, guiding the University through a difficult period in the early sixteenth century. Fisher's personality had attracted the attention of Lady Margaret Beaufort, Countess of Richmond and mother of the King, and with her assistance he was able to carry out a number of reforms and improvements, for Lady Margaret was extremely rich and anxious to perform good works. She intended leaving her large fortune to the Abbey of Westminster, but she was persuaded by Fisher to consider founding a college instead. It is to the combination of the royal lady and the humbly-born churchman that Cambridge owes not one but two colleges, and Fisher's influence probably also prompted Henry VII to recommence the building of King's College Chapel.

In 1505 Lady Margaret and Fisher founded the first of their two colleges, Christ's, just outside Barnwell Gate, where there already was a small college. God's House had been created over sixty years previously to provide more grammar teachers, and it occupied part of the site soon

Three college gate houses. King Edward's Tower at Trinity, top left. Queens' seen from St Catharine's, bottom left. Jesus with the approach known as the "Chimney".

taken over for King's College. A new site and a new charter were provided, but it was never a very prosperous college and Fisher was easily able to persuade Lady Margaret to reconstitute God's House as Christ's College, on a much larger scale with a Master, twelve Fellows and a large number of pupil-scholars, nearly half of whom were to come from the north of England. For geographical reasons Cambridge attracted scholars from the north of England and East Anglia. Oxford was more easily accessible to those from the west and south.

The original buildings were taken over and others added, including a new hall and new Master's Lodge, where Lady Margaret herself could live when she was in Cambridge. The chapel was enlarged and provided with an interior window opening from the Master's Lodge, for Margaret's own use. The College looks very different now, as it was refaced with limestone in the eighteenth century and the hall was rebuilt again in the 1870's. There are, however, three prominent remains of Lady Margaret's building. On the outside of the gatehouse, over the beautiful original door, is a magnificent and highly coloured display of heraldry in relief, showing the Foundress's arms supported by two yales (a yale was a mythical beast with an antelope's body, goat's head and feet, elephant's tail and horns pointing in different directions). Inside the court is a further manifestation of Tudor flamboyant advertisement in the oriel of the Master's Lodge, which has a smaller coloured relief of Lady Margaret's arms and yales. Thirdly and best of all, some side windows in the chapel contain stained glass belonging to the days of God's House. This is some of the oldest glass in Cambridge, almost certainly made by the King's glaziers and more than thirty years older than the glass in King's Chapel.

Almost immediately Lady Margaret wished to found a second college, this time not by adding to an existing one but by closing down a run-down religious house and converting it into a college (much as Bishop Alcock had done at Jesus). The hospital of St John, in the centre of the town, had been founded as a place where the sick and aged could be cared for and it was run by Augustinian monks. It had been the place where in 1280 Bishop Hugh de Balsham had made his abortive attempt to place some scholars. By the early sixteenth century its work was unsatisfactory and it needed renovating. Fisher considered that it could, if suitably re-endowed, be used to provide more accommodation for the University.

In 1509 Lady Margaret made a preliminary agreement to found the new college but unfortunately she died the same year without making any provision for it in her will. It took Fisher two years to get consent from, among others, the Pope, the Bishop of Ely and King Henry VIII to suppress the old foundation and to start the new, which would bear the same dedication to St John the Evangelist. A splendid new college court arose, following the plan established at Queens', with tall gate tower, hall, Master's Lodge and library incorporated, all of brick dressed with stone. Only the fine late thirteenth century chapel was retained.

Lady Margaret's first college, Christ's: the gateway with her arms above and the fine original doors.

The court shared two features of its sister foundation: the gateway had an even more splendid display of Tudor heraldry but with a more liberal sprinkling of daisies (marguerites, in rememberence of Margaret), and the Master's Lodge had a similarly decorated oriel window (which is now built into the Victorian Master's Lodge and overlooks the Master's garden). In spite of dying before the foundation actually took place, Margaret is considered the true founder of St John's, and so her badge has place of honour and her portrait hangs above high table in the hall.

St John's was a large college with fifty Fellows, and by mid-century had become the largest in Cambridge with over one hundred and fifty members. It was soon to be the most influential college in Cambridge which itself was on the point of becoming one of the most influential towns in the kingdom.

The Reformation and Trinity

It was not only by new buildings that John Fisher left his mark on Cambridge. His genius for organisation and his sympathy with moderate reform had resulted in, among other things, the establishment of the Lady Margaret Professorship of Divinity in 1502 (he became the first Professor). Fisher persuaded the great Dutch scholar Erasmus to stay in Cambridge for the years 1510-13. The early sixteenth century was a crucial time for the dissemination of ideas on religion, and the part played by Erasmus was vital. He was the first to teach Greek in the University and he was engaged on textual criticism of the Bible, both highly unpopular activities in some circles, but encouraging to those in sympathy with the new learning. Erasmus, through Fisher's influence, became Professor of Divinity in 1511 and so had a platform from which to reach scholars throughout the University. Clearly there was going to

Lady Margaret's second college, St John's: the marguerites and forget-me-nots are in honour of Margaret whose motto was "Souvent me souvient". St John the Evangelist with eagle is above.

be much argument between the adherents of traditional doctrines and those who were willing to think along new lines.

Caxton had printed his first book in 1471. Ideas could reach England from the continent quickly. Although Fisher felt that some reform of Church and University was desirable, his religious views were highly orthodox. He would not be a party to heresy, and so as Chancellor he supervised the public burning of Luther's books as heretical.

An important centre for reformers in Cambridge was the house of the Augustinian Friars, which stood just behind Bene't Street. Lutheran doctrine began to spread in Germany through other Augustinian Friars and soon reached the order's house in Cambridge. There, one of the leaders was Robert Barnes, who became Prior in 1523 but who was convicted of heresy following a sermon he preached two years later. He and other like-minded people met in the White Horse Inn in what is now King's Parade, among them Thomas Bilney, Hugh Latimer (Fellows of Trinity Hall and Clare respectively), Miles Coverdale, another Augustinian, and William Tyndale, who had left Oxford where the Church was not so favourable for reform. The new doctrines were studied and discussed, and sermons were preached in Great St Mary's and in particular in St Edward's Church, where both Trinity Hall and Clare used aisles as their college chapels. Bilney was burned at the stake in Norwich in 1531, and Barnes at Smithfield in 1540, after repeated convictions for heresy.

In the middle of these discussions of religion came the question of the King's divorce from Katherine of Aragon. The University wavered, compromised and with some misgivings gave a muted consent, thereby escaping almost certain penalties. But Chancellor John Fisher would not agree, and remained a steadfast opponent of the divorce. Like Sir Thomas More he was arrested, tried and executed in 1535 and later canonised. Fisher was succeeded as Chancellor by Thomas Cromwell, and at once Papal authority gave way to that of the King.

A further consequence of the divorce was the dissolution of the monasteries. In Cambridge this resulted in the closure of the wealthy Barnwell Priory, monastic Buckingham College and all the houses of friars. This last was a particularly hard blow as friars had been deeply involved with teaching and their houses also contained many students. The University suffered a severe loss of resources so that Robert Ascham, Princess Elizabeth's tutor, could refer to it as "this destitute and unhappy University". Even the creation by Henry VIII in 1540 of five Regius Professorships of Divinity, Civil Law, Physic, Hebrew and Greek, and the founding of Magdalene College where Buckingham College had been, did not improve matters greatly. The Regius Professorships may have been Henry's way of thanking the University for its support over his divorce, but they did little for the colleges. Things might have got even worse if the King's 1545 Act for the Dissolution of Collegiate Foundations had been carried out, for it would have involved

The pulpit in St Edward's Church from which Ridley and Latimer preached the Reformation.

The courts of St John's, leading towards the Bridge of Sighs. The arms are those of the Countess of Shrewsbury, a benefactress.

all Cambridge's colleges. However, former Cambridge men in high positions at court were able to persuade the King to issue a commission to Matthew Parker, the Vice-Chancellor, and others to report on the revenues and numbers of students in the colleges. The report was favourable and, being persuaded by Queen Katharine Parr that the University could usefully provide clergy for his new Church, Henry decided not only to spare the colleges but to found another one himself. Earlier Henry had converted Wolsey's Cardinal College at Oxford into the even more splendid Christ Church. Now at Cambridge he was to create another great college, Trinity.

Trinity was not exactly a new college. It was created from the two earlier foundations King's Hall and Michaelhouse, which stood close to one

45

another on the present site of Trinity. King's Hall occupied the area west of the Great Gate and the present chapel. Michaelhouse was founded earlier, it was more modest in scale and probably occupied the south-west side of the present Great Court. The King's Hall scholars came from well-connected families and had ambitions to the higher posts in the Church or State. Michaelhouse scholars came from humbler origins and tended to become country clergy. When Henry VIII came to found his new college it was appropriate that he should use King's Hall as a basis, especially as Edward III was a crucial figure in Henry's ancestry. The King amalgamated the two foundations and named the new college Trinity. He appointed his Chaplain, John Redman, the former Warden of King's Hall, as its first Master.

At the time of the re-foundation in 1546, King's Hall had already grown to two courts, with two gatehouses, King Edward's Tower leading to the original court and a new gatehouse, the Great Gate, which had not long been finished. The Great Gate became the formal entrance to the new College, and was therefore adorned with heraldry which at first appears out-of-date, but which turns out to be yet another reference by the Tudors to their noble ancestry. For the royal arms are those of Edward III and underneath those of his six sons, who included the Black Prince, and the Dukes of York and Lancaster, from whom descended the two branches who fought the Wars of the Roses. Henry VIII claimed descent from both. One of Edward's sons has a blank shield, because he died as a baby before he had been granted arms.

Henry quadrupled the revenues of the original colleges by making further grants of money and land from former monasteries. He gave the buildings of the Franciscan Friary to provide materials for further works. Trinity also inherited the water supply that the Franciscans had obtained for themselves in 1327 and which now supplies the fountain in Great Court. The new College was therefore very well endowed. From the start it was a large college, with a Master (who was to be appointed by the Crown), fifty graduate Fellows and ten Scholars (the first incumbents were nominated by Henry), forty Grammar Scholars (who soon became undergraduates) and eight Bible Clerks. It may be that the King intended to carry out grand improvements to the existing buildings, comparable to those Henry VI had planned for King's, or Wolsey for his college at Oxford, but he died very shortly after the foundation. Many harsh things have been said of Henry VIII, but Cambridge ought to be eternally grateful to him for the five Regius Professorships, for the completion of King's Chapel and for the creation of Trinity.

The new College received its first statutes from Henry's son Edward VI. There was as yet no Great Court. Elizabethan maps of Cambridge show that the buildings of King's Hall and Michaelhouse extended over a wide area broken up into smaller courts by ranges built over the past one hundred and fifty years. But the germ was there and it only awaited a far-sighted Master to bring Great Court into being.

The Great Gate of Trinity: Henry VIII presides over the shields of Edward III and his sons. Henry's sceptre is now a chair-leg, an undergraduate joke that has become a tradition.

Elizabethan Protestantism

Religious troubles were far from over with the swing to Protestantism in the reigns of Henry VIII and his young son Edward VI. The founding of Trinity and the refounding of Magdalene College did much to restore the confidence of the University, but it was still impoverished.

Originally the colleges had been founded for senior members, teachers who were almost all in holy orders, but in the sixteenth century more and more colleges took in undergraduates too. These were pensioners who were expected to pay the college for their keep and tuition, with a small number of sizars who paid little or nothing but were expected to perform menial duties instead. By the middle of the century it became fashionable for young men from well-to-do families to enrol as members of colleges, but with very little intention of reading for degrees. From that time until well into the twentieth century Cambridge, like Oxford, had a proportion of such young men. In some periods they were more dominant but they gave the University a reputation for idle privilege it did not really deserve. There was always a majority who were eager to advance their careers and many of Cambridge's most distinguished men were to start their academic life as sizars.

The work of Church reform continued in Cambridge. Twelve out of thirteen compilers of the English Prayer Book of 1549 were Cambridge scholars, but there was a set-back in 1553 when Mary, a Catholic, succeeded her young half-brother, Edward VI, the zealous Protestant. Cambridge briefly found itself the centre of interest as Mary went first to Sawston Hall, only a few miles away, and from there to other Catholic houses in Suffolk. The Regent, the Duke of Northumberland, pursued her as far as Cambridge, where he proclaimed Lady Jane Grey as Queen. He persuaded Vice-Chancellor Sandys to join him, but soon they were compelled to change their tune and proclaim Mary. Their change of heart came too late, however, and both were arrested and sent to the Tower of London, where Northumberland was executed. Sandys was released: he later became Archbishop of York. Life was indeed uncertain for those in high places.

Under Mary, England and Cambridge reverted to Catholicism, at least openly. At a public ceremony the bodies of the two German reformers Martin Bucer and Paul Fagius, who had died in Cambridge, were exhumed, their coffins chained to stakes and burnt on Market Hill. Great St Mary's and St Michael's Churches, where they had been buried, were ritually purified.

Two years later in 1555 came an even greater shock to Cambridge, the burning at Oxford of Hugh Latimer and Nicholas Ridley, followed soon afterwards by that of Thomas Cranmer, all of them Fellows of Cambridge colleges who had been prominent in the reform movement. Cambridge itself witnessed one burning when John Hullier, a preacher at King's Lynn and a former member of King's College, met his end on Jesus

Tudor chimneys in Trinity Lane.

*Jesus Green, the site of
Cambridge's only martyrdom.
John Hullier was burnt here on
Maundy Thursday, 1556.*

Green. The local people were filled with sympathy and revulsion and
collected pieces of his bones as relics.

The accession of Elizabeth brought back Protestantism once again and
the new religion became more and more deeply entrenched. The attitude
of the University may be summed up in the actions of a Vice-Chancellor
of the day, Andrew Perne, Master of Peterhouse. Perne was required to
preside over the burning of the German reformers' bodies but only three
years later he felt able to take charge of the service of rehabilitation when
their ashes were reburied. One relic of Andrew Perne is the weather vane
on the spire of St Peter's Church on Castle Hill, originally at Peterhouse
but put in its present place by the antiquary William Cole in the
eighteenth century. The initials "AP" can be clearly seen; in the sixteenth
century it was remarked that they stood for "A Papist" or "A Protestant"
or even "A Puritan", according to the direction of the wind. This is
somewhat unfair to Perne, who did a great deal for his college and whose
actions as Vice-Chancellor probably saved the University (and perhaps
the town) from severe penalties.

During the long reign of Elizabeth, Cambridge's fortunes rose. For nearly forty years the Chancellor was Elizabeth's great minister William Cecil, Lord Burghley, a former member of St John's and under his guidance the University, like the nation, prospered. He encouraged the new religion while discouraging extremists, and he tightened University control over discipline and administration.

There were other great men who remembered their University and used their influence to help. Several were from St John's, the most influential college before the rise of Trinity. These included Roger Ascham, who had been tutor to Elizabeth, and John Cheke, the first Regius Professor of Greek. But perhaps the two who exerted the greatest influence after William Cecil were Matthew Parker and John Whitgift, Masters of Corpus Christi and Trinity Colleges respectively, and later in succession Archbishops of Canterbury.

Matthew Parker, the son of a Norwich cloth manufacturer, became a student and fellow of Corpus Christi, then chaplain to Henry VIII who proposed him as Master and then Vice Chancellor. Elizabeth wished to make him Archbishop of Canterbury, but he was then over fifty and reluctant to take on the onerous task. The Queen and Burghley were determined and he gave way saying that he might not persuade people through his personality but he might hope to do so by his pen. He used his abilities and integrity to make the Church of England a tolerant and enlightened institution.

He is best remembered in Cambridge, for rescuing many rare manuscripts, mainly from the dispersed libraries of the dissolved monasteries. Bibles, theological and historical writings, editions of the classical authors, Chaucer and others, many with superb illustrations, came into his hands, and the bulk of them passed to Corpus Christi. The most valuable is the sixth century Gospel of St Luke, almost certainly brought to England by St Augustine, which is taken to the inauguration ceremony of each Archbishop of Canterbury guarded by two Fellows.

John Whitgift was a more formidable personality than Parker and perhaps more respected than loved, both in Cambridge and Canterbury. He had been a dedicated and hard working Master and Regius Professor of Divinity, and here again the Queen could discern the right man for the task. His insistence on upholding the doctrine of the Established Church had a steadying effect on the Church and Cambridge.

The Queen, doubtless prompted by her Cambridge-educated courtiers took an interest in the University, and she paid a visit to Cambridge in 1564. She lodged in King's College and spent several active days listening to sermons, disputations, plays, orations and addresses, replying in Latin or Greek, and conversing in Latin with scholars in the colleges she visited. She must have enjoyed her visit, especially the college plays.

The plays performed for the Queen were not great literature, but they established the interest which led up to the great theatre soon to follow. Scholars were familiar with Latin comedies and tragedies but English drama was only just emerging. The second oldest surviving comedy, "Gammer Gurton's Needle", was performed at Christ's College in about 1554. It has an obvious plot and contains much slapstick and crude doggerel. University writers did a great deal to prepare the way and some were well known in England by the turn of the century: Robert Greene, Thomas Nashe, John Fletcher and, most brilliant of all, Christopher Marlowe. All were educated in Cambridge.

The first press in Cambridge was set up in 1521-2 by John Siberch who came from Cologne and was a friend of Erasmus. On his travels for the family printing business he met Richard Croke from Cambridge. Croke seems to have instigated the setting up of Siberch's press in Cambridge. Despite a loan of £20 from the University and publishing a number of books, the business was not a success and he returned to Cologne. In 1534 the University received "Letters Patent" from Henry VIII to "print and sell all manner of books", but no printing was done until 1584 when continuous publication started.

The University was now closely involved with the nation's life and culture. Apart from an interest in the theatre a Renaissance gentleman was expected to be poet and musician as well as soldier, courtier and administrator. The outstanding example is Sir Philip Sidney, who went to both Oxford and Cambridge but did not take a degree. Henry VIII had composed songs and dances. Poetry and music were lively interests in Elizabethan Cambridge and a great poet appeared before long.

Edmund Spenser entered Pembroke College as a sizar in 1569, and for some years he struggled to adapt his poetry to the fashionable craze for rigid Latin models quite unsuitable for English. He broke away and became a major influence in establishing a native tradition of lyrical and narrative verse. His greatest work, *The Faerie Queen* fused the style of fairy-tale romance with the aspirations of Elizabethan England into an exotic fantasy. When he died he was regarded as England's greatest poet.

What of the town itself during this century of religious and academic reform? It seems that the townspeople followed the country in adopting the new religion but otherwise had changed little, remaining largely rural. In spite of acquiring an ally in Roger, Lord North, who became Lord Lieutenant in 1569 and who entertained the Queen at his mansion at Kirtling, the citizens of Cambridge were still under the dominance of the University. They resented more than anything the University's interference in their leisure activities: football, bear-baiting, cock-fighting, play acting, all fell under University bans. In the sixteenth century, for almost the first time, the University produced men recognisable as individuals. We often have portraits of them. This distinction did not extend to townsfolk.

51

Chapter 4

Town sites
University sites

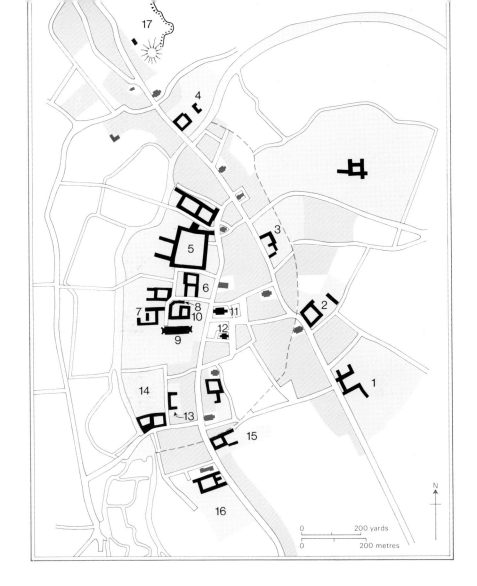

The Gate of Honour, Gonville and Caius College. Students walked through the gate to receive their degrees in the Senate House.

Middle Ages to Renaissance

The ideas of the Italian Renaissance had spread to France before 1500, but England's religious problems ensured that an architecture based on that of Rome took a long time to arrive. In Cambridge, as elsewhere in England, the first signs of it are visible not in buildings but in decorations and ornaments. Details of Roman style buildings appear in some of the glass in King's College Chapel, from about 1515, and twenty years later in details of carvings on the screen, but none of it was done by English craftsmen. What little building there was early in the century consisted largely of adaptation rather than new works.

Even when Dr John Caius obtained a charter in 1557 to refound and enlarge his old College, fourteenth century Gonville Hall, his new buildings were still mediaeval in form. Caius came from Norwich (his name seems to have been Keys originally, later Latinised without changing the pronunciation); he studied ancient languages, later took up medicine in Padua, where he qualified as a doctor, and travelled in Italy

53

and France before returning to England to become physician to Edward VI and Queen Mary in succession. He returned to Cambridge, became Master of Gonville and remained a staunch Catholic, even under Elizabeth. Caius established the College's pre-eminence in medical studies. William Harvey who discovered the circulation of the blood was a graduate of the College.

His new court consisted of only three ranges of buildings, with the fourth side closed by a wall with a gateway, for he considered this arrangement more healthy than the traditional closed court as it allowed fresh air to enter. The originality of Caius' architectural additions to his College lay in his three gateways, designed to symbolise the progress of the student through college life. The first, the Gate of Humility, has simple fluted pilasters on either side of an arch. The Gate when built was in Trinity Street but is now in the Master's garden (Caius would have enjoyed the irony). The second, inscribed to Virtue on the outer side and to Wisdom on the inner, takes the form of a classical building with orders of pilasters and a pediment. It is wholly unlike typical Elizabethan architecture. Nikolaus Pevsner calls it "historically one of the most important buildings of its date [1567] in England". It was so far ahead of its time that it inspired no imitations in Cambridge.

The Gate of Honour, on the other hand, is a endearing mixture of classical and mediaeval: Gothic arch, Corinthian columns, and round-headed niches, surmounted by a hexagonal turret with domed top and a profusion of obelisks and finials. In his exuberance and his love of conceits Caius showed himself a true Elizabethan.

Apart from Caius there is little building that is either in the classical style or indeed very grand. The main gateway to Magdalene, built about 1585, is a solitary exception, with its fine Tuscan pilasters and decorated frieze. The two colleges founded towards the end of the century, Emmanuel in 1584 and Sidney Sussex twelve years later, both on the sites of former houses of friars, were very much in the traditional manner. Both followed Caius' example and consisted of two three-sided courts each, open to one side, and they contained the usual mediaeval components, hall, chapel and Master's Lodge. Their builder was Ralph Symons of Westminster and what remains of his work shows him to be more of a master mason than an architect. Symons also built Second Court at St John's and the Hall and Master's Lodge of Trinity, all solid well-built constructions but with little attempt at originality.

Emmanuel was founded by Sir Walter Mildmay, formerly of Christ's, who had filled several positions at Elizabeth's court, including Chancellor of the Exchequer. He was above all a staunch Puritan and in his zeal to break away from the Catholic past he deliberately converted the former chapel of the Dominicans into the new College's hall and parlour, and at the same time he created an austere chapel, aligned north-south, from what may have been the friars' refectory. Puritanism had a growing number of advocates in the University; both Emmanuel

The initial "E" from Queen Elizabeth I's charter authorising Sir Walter Mildmay to found Emmanuel College in 1584. The portrait of Elizabeth is probably by Nicholas Hilliard.

The Great Court of Trinity. To the left of the Great Gate are rooms once occupied by Isaac Newton. On the same staircase Thackeray, Macaulay, Lightfoot, Jebb and Frazer have had rooms.

and Sidney Sussex Colleges were founded to foster it. In the town there was an even stronger following for the Puritans.

Visually the most important event of the late Elizabethan period was the creation of the Great Court at Trinity by Thomas Nevile, Master from 1593, a favourite of Queen Elizabeth, who later made him Dean of Canterbury. Nevile was wealthy and devoted his life and fortune to the College. Trinity College had remained for its first fifty years an awkward arrangement of ranges projecting into irregular courts, following the line of long-vanished lanes, with two gate towers (one unfinished) that led into incomplete courts and with no sense of unity. Nevile set about converting this haphazard assortment into one large unified court. It involved moving King Edward's Tower back some twenty metres, stone by stone, so that it was roughly in line with the chapel. It became a gate tower defending nothing (though there are still some remaining parts of King's Hall behind it), but it adds variety and dignity to the north side of Great Court. It is remarkable that nearly three hundred years ago it was not only possible to carry out this laborious task and to recreate the Tower in its former beauty, but that it was also thought important to do so. Conservation is no new thing. When the Tower was rebuilt the statue of Edward III was added and so probably was the unmediaeval lantern at the top, though the present one is a Victorian replacement.

The Great Gate thus became the rightful entrance to Great Court, the largest gate tower in Cambridge leading into the largest court in either Oxford or Cambridge. The significance of Henry VIII's statue and the heraldry of Edward III remained just as valid in Elizabeth's day, perhaps even more so with the successor to Elizabeth very much in mind. On the inside statues of James I, his Queen and Prince Charles commemorate royal visits in 1615, the year when Nevile died. On the south side of Great Court Nevile erected a third gate, Queen's Gate, containing a statue of Queen Elizabeth. There is no escaping the royal connections of Trinity.

Projecting ranges, some in fact not very old, were pulled down and others erected to make the four-sided court as it is today. Ralph Symons was employed to enlarge the Master's Lodge, which has, however, been much altered. Symons also built the Great Hall, on the site of the former kitchens. The former Michaelhouse hall was on the south side of the present hall; the present screens passage probably belonged to it and still has its original doorways. Nevile paid for the hall, the largest in Cambridge; it is entirely mediaeval in character, with a hammer-beam roof, large bay windows and some very fine panelling, particularly at the high-table end. It must have been considered old-fashioned even when it was built, although there are signs of the new taste in the strap decoration of the porch, in some details of the panelling and in the elegant hexagonal lantern to take off fumes from the brazier which stood in the centre and

The Great Hall of Trinity, arranged for a Christmas dinner. The massive hammer-beam roof has seen nearly 400 years of feasts.

Seventeenth century Renaissance, but still influenced by Gothic. The entrance gateway of Clare College, above, and Peterhouse chapel, below, both of the 1630's.

which provided all the hall's heating until the nineteenth century. More strap-work appears on the large fountain in the centre of the court.

Great Court is still in essence a mediaeval achievement. It is neither square nor rectangular, the paths are not symmetrical and none of the gate towers are centrally placed in their ranges. There is a constant change of building heights, and the two porches to hall and lodge are at different levels. The Court is, in fact, a typical rambling mediaeval structure that seems to have grown with little apparent unity, unless it be the use of stone throughout, for there is a marked contrast with the brick courts of St John's.

After Great Court Nevile was still not satisfied and funded the construction of the second court which bears his name. The Court was later enlarged, the two side wings have been greatly altered and the far side, a wall with a gate, removed. The original gate with strap-work and Tuscan columns can still be seen, serving as a back entrance to the College from Trinity Lane.

Gradually the hostels which had accommodated undergraduates since the very early days of the University were closing. All students were soon housed in the colleges and several were obliged to erect extra buildings to provide rooms. St John's built a second court around the turn of the century and other colleges followed suit soon afterwards. Usually these new buildings were in the traditional style, as at Pembroke and Emmanuel, but others attempted something more classical in form. The Fellows' Building at Christ's is a particularly good example, with three storeys, alternating triangular and segmental pediments on the dormer windows, and rustication surrounding the ground floor windows.

Two further buildings show the ambivalence in Cambridge to the new forms of architecture. In 1632 a new chapel, ordered by the Master, Dr Wren, was consecrated at Peterhouse (until then the College had used Little St Mary's Church). It is a curious mixture of old and new motifs: Gothic arches, niches for statues (but with shell tops behind), Perpendicular tracery, ogee arches, pilasters, pediments, polygonal turrets, strap-work and cherub figures.

Secondly, Clare College began the complete rebuilding of its fourteenth century accommodation in 1638. The style chosen for the east range is classical but the entrance gateway contains a mixture of styles, very similar to those at Peterhouse. The entrance arch has a fan vault, probably the last example in Cambridge before the Gothic Revival more than two hundred years later. Clare's rebuilding was less than half finished when the Civil War came and all work had to stop.

Elizabethan Enrichment

The reign of Elizabeth saw many changes in Cambridge, which was not surprising bearing in mind the changes in England as a whole. The University had always produced administrators and officials of state, but they now took an increasingly prominent part in public life. Numbers grew and with the extra income from the large number of pensioners, the colleges became more prosperous. The senior members and the wealthy young men now resident sought greater comfort than the colleges had originally offered, and this was reflected in the quality and quantity of food and drink, furniture and the decoration of college rooms, the appearance of portraits of prominent scholars in college halls, and in entertainments, such as the Latin plays performed on special occasions, and in music. The larger colleges had choirs with organists. There are records of local boys singing in college choirs, the most famous being Orlando Gibbons, who sang in King's College and who later became a member of the Chapel Royal, organist at Westminster Abbey and one of England's leading composers. His father had been leader of the town waits.

College gardens began to be developed in Elizabeth's reign although it is difficult to be precise since there are few records. There must have been gardens early in the University's history, but they would have been utilitarian, providing vegetables and fruit, and herbs for medicinal purposes. It is known that some monasteries had gardens as early as the twelfth century and the orchards of Ely were particularly famous. In the early sixteenth century formal gardens became the fashion. Tudor gardens were geometric in form incorporating mazes and dials. Wolsey took great interest in the design and planting of the gardens at Hampton Court. Thomas More was also renowned for his garden at Chelsea.

In 1526 William Turner, who came to be called "the Father of English Botany", entered Pembroke College. In 1538 he published *The Names of Herbs*, the earliest botanical book to come from Cambridge. He was strongly drawn to the new religion and, after crossing the authorities in Oxford for preaching without a licence, decided to travel in Europe where he made a large collection of dried plants. Turner constructed an impressive garden at Kew of his own. His *A New Herbal* was produced in installments from 1551 and completed in 1568. There are records of a number of men coming to Cambridge at that time to study plants and write books on husbandry.

The growing interest in nature and increased leisure made gardens places for recreation as well as relaxation. The game of bowls was known in the Middle Ages and it became popular in the colleges. A bowling green still survives behind the old King's Hall range of Trinity College. Other games included rough football, often an excuse for a free fight between scholars of different colleges. The University eventually laid down regulations against intercollegiate games.

The herb garden of Emmanuel. The hall to the left has buttresses dating from when it was the chapel of the Black Friars.

The oldest existing college bridge over the Cam, at Clare College. It cost £284 in 1639.

Colleges backing on to the river built bridges to enable their members to use walks and gardens on the west side. These bridges were mainly wooden, but King's had already built a stone one by 1627. It was fortunate that, as the river was liable to flood, most of the low-lying land to the west had not been used by the town. Interest in the river and the desire to maintain open spaces across it have led to one of the most striking features of Cambridge, the Backs. A Cambridge college today is unthinkable without its lawns, gardens and tree walks, all of which came into being at the end of the sixteenth and early seventeenth centuries. Perhaps because of this Cambridge did not provide a Botanic Garden until much later, although Oxford's dates from 1621.

The ideal of the complete Renaissance man was not far from a student's thoughts and music was of increasing importance. Unaccompanied choral music could be heard every day in college chapels and there must have been much private music making. Elizabethans delighted in madrigals, catches and songs with accompaniment and in playing the lute, virginals and viols. Thomas Campion, who was at Peterhouse in the 1580's, illustrates this ideal man very well. He became a physician, but he also wrote lyrics with music and he was an accomplished lutenist.

At this time England was one of Europe's leading centres for music, with composers of the stature of Tallis, Byrd, Dowland and Gibbons. Much of their music was for dancing, which was very popular with Elizabethans from the Queen and her court down. Her countrymen came to be called "the dancing English".

In the early seventeenth century more poets came to Cambridge. George Herbert was a Fellow of Trinity for some years before moving on to a political career in London and eventually to a quiet rectory near Salisbury. Herbert's poetry consists entirely of religious lyrics; several are still in use as hymns. Robert Herrick, another Cambridge poet, wrote love poetry, though he too became a country clergyman. Later there came a whole host of poets known today for one or two poems that have won unchallengeable places in anthologies: Edmund Waller of King's, Sir John Suckling and Richard Lovelace, both of Trinity, and Richard Crashaw of Peterhouse. Andrew Marvell was at Trinity as a sizar before he left to take over family property at Meldreth.

But the greatest writer to come to Cambridge in the seventeenth century was without question John Milton. His seriousness and his knowledge of languages were already apparent when he arrived at Christ's in 1625, and because of his delicate good looks he was soon known as the "Lady of Christ's". He took part in college life, but was not popular with his fellow students. He was decidedly Puritan and made attacks on both King and

Singing on the river at Trinity. The choir still sings madrigals by Orlando Gibbons, who once performed in King's College Chapel nearby.

The "dancing English" on Parker's Piece. In the background is Park Terrace, one of the finest late Georgian terraces in the city.

clergy, but he built up a reputation as a Latin scholar and as a poet in Latin and English. One of his best early poems, *On the Morning of Christ's Nativity*, was written during his years at Cambridge, and his friendship with Edward King inspired the great elegy *Lycidas* a few years afterwards. Milton, like Bacon before him and others after, was disappointed with the outmoded curriculum and low standards of scholarship.

Two other writers deserve a mention. Thomas Fuller was at Queens' and Sidney Sussex before he became curate at St Bene't's. He wrote the first history of the University but is better known for *The Worthies of England*, in which many interesting anecdotes have been preserved. Jeremy Taylor was born the son of a Cambridge barber, and was one of the first pupils at the school founded by Dr Stephen Perse of Caius. Taylor went to Caius, where he became a Fellow and eventually Bishop of Down. His devotional books *Holy Living* and *Holy Dying* were extremely popular in the seventeenth century.

The Civil War and Recovery

The University was confident during the early years of the seventeenth century. The patronage of James I gave security, and there was an increase in numbers, reflected in new buildings. But in many colleges the religious question simmered underneath. The strong Puritan element was centred around Emmanuel College. Under their first Master, Laurence Chaderton, Emmanuel became one of the largest colleges, although the Puritans were still a minority in the University. Chaderton was Master for thirty-eight years before resigning: he eventually died in 1640 aged 102, as can be seen from his tombstone in the College Chapel.

In despair of finding a religious climate where Puritanism could flourish, a great many emigrated to new colonies in America. So many came from Emmanuel that New England was sometimes referred to as "Emmanuel's Land". Amongst them was John Harvard who gave his library, money, and half his estate to the college founded in Cambridge, Massachusetts, which bears his name.

The town was still very much under the control of the University, but that did not prevent a considerable degree of prosperity. There was money to be made from the University and the wealthy students now attending it. Between 1610 and 1614 a group of well-to-do citizens undertook a project to bring fresh water into the town to a conduit on Market Hill. Parts of it are still visible: the open watercourse in Trumpington Road, the small streams running along the gutters in Trumpington Street and the attractive conduit itself, now resited at the corner of Lensfield Road. Although he was only one of those responsible, it became known as Hobson's Conduit after Thomas Hobson, a prominent citizen who owned the George Inn and carried on a business as a carrier and horse hirer. From Hobson's habit of compelling would-be hirers of horses to take the one which had rested longest comes the expression "Hobson's Choice", or no choice at all. Hobson's death was the subject of two indifferent poems by John Milton.

The religious rift between town and University widened early in the reign of Charles I. Puritanism had become popular among the townspeople, perhaps because of the University's tendency to support the King and the established Church. In 1610 town sermons were instituted in Holy Trinity Church and these continued until the mid-eighteenth century. The brilliant Duke of Buckingham became Chancellor and the influence of Archbishop Laud was manifest in the more elaborate High Church ritual appearing in some college chapels, notably the newly built Peterhouse Chapel.

When matters came to a head between King Charles and Parliament there was no doubt about where sympathies lay: the University was for the King, the town for Parliament. East Anglia was Parliamentarian, and early in the Civil War, in 1642, formed the Eastern Counties Association, which had its headquarters at Cambridge. This

The Fellows' Garden at Clare and the Head Gardener. The river flows between the garden and the back of the College.

The rush for lectures in Trumpington Street. Water for Hobson's Conduit still flows beside the pavements.

Association was created as a means of defence against the King's soldiers, and it included Oliver Cromwell. Cromwell came from a Huntingdonshire family and was rapidly becoming respected in the country as a leader and administrator. In 1616 he had spent a year as a fellow commoner at Sidney Sussex College, leaving on the death of his father. In 1640 Cromwell was chosen as Member of Parliament for Cambridge and when hostilities began in 1642 he became virtually a dictator in East Anglia.

At the request of the King, the colleges collected their plate for dispatch to York to provide funds for the royal cause. Most of it was intercepted by Cromwell. Colleges had accumulated plate gradually as a form of reserve fund and the fact that they gave it up to the King so readily indicates the strength of their commitment and their fear of Puritanism.

The colleges ordered weapons to be delivered for their defence but most of these were also secured by the town.

The Civil War period was to be a trying time for the University. Under an Order for the Regulation of the Universities almost all the Anglican heads of colleges were ejected and replaced by Puritan sympathisers, often men of no great learning. Over a hundred and eighty Fellows were also ejected including Abraham Cowley, the poet. Men suspected of being Royalists were kept under surveillance. Numbers in colleges were severely depleted, so that the University could carry on only with great difficulty. In 1643 Cambridge was used as a garrison under Edward Montague, Earl of Manchester, another Huntingdonshire man who had also been at Sidney Sussex College. Soldiers were quartered in the college buildings, even in King's College Chapel, and the fortifications of the former castle were strengthened. Much of the stonework has long since gone for college building, but the remains of the extra bastions constructed can still be seen to the rear of Shire Hall. College bridges over the Cam were pulled down. The precautions turned out to be needless: there was no danger to Cambridge, no battles were fought nearby, and the garrison was dispersed.

In 1643 Parliament passed an ordinance providing for the demolition of monuments of a superstitious or idolatrous nature and William Dowsing was instructed to supervise the destruction of statues and images. At Pembroke he "broke ten cherubims and pulled down eighty superstitious pictures", at Peterhouse he tore down "two mighty great angels with wings" and at Queens' he destroyed over a hundred more pictures. Even Holy Trinity Church with a congregation wholly of townspeople suffered.

It seems that churches and chapels which had gained a reputation for High Church activities suffered most. Other places escaped, including King's College Chapel, in which only a few small stone carvings were mutilated. It is not clear exactly how the great stained glass windows survived. Perhaps it was because the Provost Benjamin Whichcote was a moderate Puritan and respected by Cromwell, perhaps the townspeople had already developed an affection for the chapel.

In 1644 the use of Greek, Latin and Hebrew in sermons was forbidden. The Long Parliament was even contemplating the closing down of Oxford and Cambridge completely, but they were saved by Cromwell's dismissal of Parliament. Cromwell was now Lord Protector and John Milton spent the entire Commonwealth period as Cromwell's Latin Secretary, writing political letters and tracts. The time spent in the service of his country postponed the fulfillment of what he knew was his great destiny as an epic poet.

The Restoration of the King in 1660 came as a relief to the country as a whole and in particular to the universities. Bonfires were lit in Cambridge as elsewhere in England, and people shared the general

A grotesque figure carved in oak in the early seventeenth century on a house opposite Magdalene College.

rejoicing. Christ's College accounts show that a total of £3 12s 8d was paid for bonfires, music, food and beer. Charles II assured the universities that their former charters and privileges would be restored. This did not please the townspeople of Cambridge who were reluctant to return to the subordinate position that the Commonwealth had done so much to relieve. The colleges started to repair the damage of the last twenty years. Masters appointed during the Commonwealth were replaced by the rightful Masters or by new ones elected by the Fellows. Charles took a great interest in the University and was a frequent visitor, though perhaps this was because it was conveniently close to Newmarket.

Two years after the Restoration the Act of Uniformity was passed and all members of the University had to subscribe to it. Allegiance to the Church of England and an oath to observe the Thirty-nine Articles was required. Numbers of Puritan Fellows felt unable to comply, and so were compelled to leave. Although an Anglican, the famous naturalist John Ray, a Fellow of Trinity, resigned rather than accept the oaths. But the controversy on religious matters became less heated. The writings and preachings of a group of senior members of the University, known as the Cambridge Platonists, were aimed at making religious debate less virulent. The Platonists turned to the writings of Plato, with their emphasis on reasoning, rather than those of Aristotle whose works had been authoritative in the middle ages. Though the leading Platonists were inclined towards Puritanism, their approach to reason was of greater importance. "Reason is the candle of the Lord", as Benjamin Whichcote, Provost of King's, put it. The Platonists included John Smith and Ralph Cudworth, who at the age of twenty-eight was Master of Clare and Professor of Hebrew, a respected preacher, of independent mind and an outstanding scholar.

A further mollifying influence on religious controversy was the growth of interest in the natural sciences. The Royal Society was founded in 1662. The first secretary was John Wilkes, Master of Trinity, and the Society included many Cambridge men. In the University the shift away from religious traditions is revealed in the creation of Chairs of Mathematics, Astronomy and Chemistry. The natural sciences also fostered the growth of gardens. The other of Cromwell's two poet secretaries, Andrew Marvell, wrote on the peace and reason to be found in gardens. As was the fashion, college gardens were laid out in formal rectangles with hedges divided by walks. Many new trees and plants were introduced, such as tulips, nasturtiums and laburnums.

There were no active writers or poets at Cambridge during the Restoration period. The greatest poet of the day, John Dryden, was indeed a Cambridge man, but he was at Trinity during the Commonwealth and he apparently wrote nothing of significance then. His great antagonist Thomas Shadwell had been at Caius at about the same time. Samuel Pepys, too, was a student at Magdalene under the Commonwealth.

The east end of Wren's chapel at Emmanuel. The lake was once the fish pond of the Black Friars.

Pepys came from a family with connections in Cambridgeshire, at Impington and Cottenham, and his diary records several visits to his old College and University. But the entries tell us very little about Cambridge, apart from the names of the inns where he lodged, the Three Tuns (where he and his companions "drank pretty hard and many healths to the King"), the Black Bear and the Rose. He seemed to enjoy visiting his old haunts but was not keen to stay long. After his death his library was given to Magdalene, where it can still be seen, the three thousand volumes all bound with Pepys' crest arranged in the bookcases which he had made for him. There are mediaeval manuscripts, editions published by Caxton, engravings, music, maps and much material on navies for the history he contemplated writing but never did. Most important of all are the six manuscript volumes of his famous diary.

As part of the move forward after the Restoration, St Catharine's began a complete rebuilding programme in 1674 and Clare College resumed the rebuilding which had been interrupted by the Civil War. But the most memorable architecture was to come from the man who has come to be regarded as England's greatest architect.

The old bridge of St John's, built by Grumbold using Wren's suggestions. It spans between the College and its grounds in the Backs.

Chapter 5

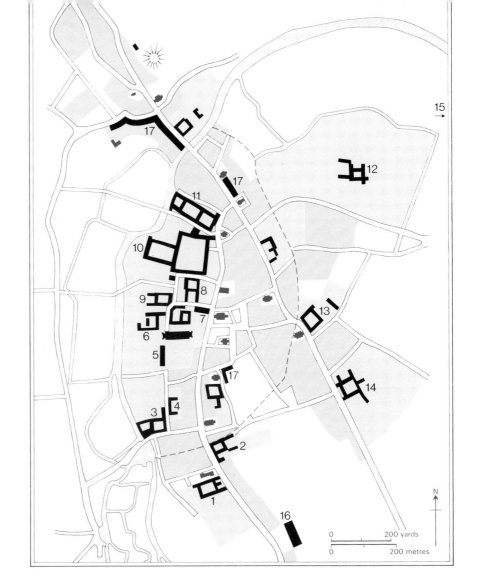

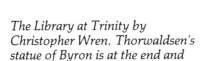

Town sites
University sites

The Library at Trinity by Christopher Wren. Thorwaldsen's statue of Byron is at the end and on each side are busts of poets, writers and scholars from all ages.

Wren's Baroque

Two figures have left their mark on Cambridge in the last years of the seventeenth century. Christopher Wren's three works are among the most beautiful of Cambridge buildings, and Isaac Newton remains arguably the greatest intellect to have emerged from the University. The two are complementary, for although both were educated in the traditional manner, both were pioneers of the new learning in the natural sciences. Newton's work on motion contains references to Wren's earlier experiments on the subject.

Christopher Wren was the son of the Chaplain to the King and Dean of Windsor who was also interested in mathematics and architecture. Wren went up to Wadham College, Oxford and showed extraordinary brilliance in almost every subject he took up, mathematics, scientific drawing, astronomy, algebraic treatises, and metrical essays in Latin. When he was twenty-five Wren became Professor of Astronomy at Gresham College, London.

Wren was a founding member when the Royal Society received its charter in 1662. The Society was founded "to make faithful records of all the works of nature and art which can come within their reach", or more simply work towards "a philosophy of mankind". Unlike now, the scope of the Royal Society covered the whole field of knowledge and it included writers like Dryden and Evelyn as well as the chemist Robert Boyle and the historian Bishop Sprat. Wren must have been among the youngest of this distinguished band.

In 1660, at the age of twenty-eight Wren had been appointed Savilian Professor of Astronomy at Oxford, a post he held for thirteen years. But his attentions were soon directed towards architecture, which was closely linked with the two subjects which had long attracted him, mathematics and geometry. By 1663 the Norman cathedral of St Paul's had been partly rebuilt many times and was in a very bad state. Through influential friends and because of the great esteem in which he was already held, Wren was appointed to the Commission for repairing it.

In the same year came commissions for buildings in both Oxford and Cambridge, from distinguished men who wanted to offer gifts to record their thanks for surviving the Civil War. In Oxford Gilbert Sheldon, Bishop of London and former Warden of All Souls College, wished to present the University with a building for University ceremonies. Wren decided on a classical theatre, based on the Theatre of Marcellus in Rome and added an ingenious roof supported by mathematically-designed trusses to span seventy feet.

At Cambridge Wren was asked by his uncle, Dr Matthew Wren, Bishop of Ely, to provide a new chapel for Matthew's former college, Pembroke. Matthew Wren had been Master of Peterhouse and he had ordered their chapel in 1632, with its curious mixture of mediaeval and Renaissance features. As a High Church follower of Archbishop Laud, Dr Wren had been deprived of his Mastership and imprisoned for eighteen years. He vowed that if he survived he would dedicate a chapel in thanks, and he chose his old college for its site. Pembroke had been the first college to have its own chapel but the old chapel, now the Old Library, was small and Dr Wren proposed something grander.

By the late seventeenth century books on classical architecture by Latin and Italian architects had been translated into English and were widely available. Christopher Wren certainly knew a number of them, and the plans for Pembroke chapel were based on a design for a Roman temple by Sebastiano Serlio. Pembroke chapel is the first truly classical building in Cambridge. The most interesting aspect of the exterior is the stone west front which faces Trumpington Street. It is simple and well balanced: one large window with niches and pilasters on each side, the surmounting pediment containing only a garlanded shield. The other sides are of brick with simple stone dressings. Inside, the chapel was originally a plain rectangle and the prevailing atmosphere is one of restraint, but there are details of great richness. The fine plaster ceiling,

Pembroke College Fellows' Garden, with the old Master's Lodge built by Alfred Waterhouse in the background.

Two hundred years of building:
The Pembroke Chapel by Wren,
residences by Waterhouse and the
Burrough's Building, Peterhouse,
built on the site of its earliest hall.

by Henry Doogood and John Grove, is exceptionally well executed and there is some good woodwork, especially the altar rails, by Cornelius Austin. Wren had the happy knack of attracting and keeping fine craftsmen.

The chapel was lengthened by George Gilbert Scott the Younger in 1880. Scott inserted a short chancel at the east end, separating it from the main part by two marble columns on each side. The chapel retains its plain glass windows and is thought to be Wren's first completed work.

A few years later Wren was back in Cambridge to build a second chapel, at Emmanuel College. Built on the former site of the Black Friars, Emmanuel's chapel was a small and extremely plain room, as befitted a Puritan foundation. At the Restoration Dr William Sancroft became

Master and it was decided to replace the humble meeting room with a grander chapel that was aligned correctly east-west. Sancroft was Dean of St Paul's when he met Wren in discussions about repairs to the Cathedral, and as a result Wren was commissioned to design the new chapel.

Emmanuel's chapel owes something to Matthew Wren's chapel at Peterhouse and like it has an arcade stretching across the court. But at Emmanuel what appears to be the chapel front is in fact false, for there is a gallery that runs the whole width of the court with a cloister walk underneath. The real chapel lies further back. The inspiration is Baroque rather than pure classical, the work of an architect now quite sure of himself. The centre bay is brought forward by the use of half-columns instead of pilasters. One of the great joys of Emmanuel is to examine the

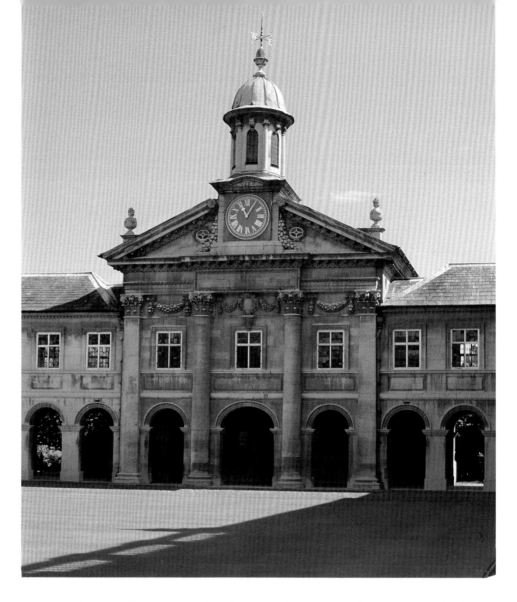

Emmanuel Chapel, above the west front, with the former Master's Gallery and cloister. Left the cloister walk under the Gallery.

beautifully conceived and executed carving in Ketton stone: the frieze, the swags between the Corinthian capitals and inside the pediment. There is a profusion of detail, but never too much to confuse the overall effect.

Simplicity is the keynote inside, but again there is a wealth of detail in wood carving and plaster; the work of the same craftsmen used by Wren in Pembroke. But unlike Pembroke the chapel is much as Wren left it, except that the plain glass windows have been replaced by Victorian portraits of men who have influenced Cambridge or been an ornament to their college, including Harvard, Chaderton and Sancroft. Sancroft had contributed largely to the cost of the chapel and later became Archbishop of Canterbury.

For the next few years Wren, by now Surveyor of His Majesty's Works, was fully occupied with his plan for London and designs for parish churches and St Paul's. The next connection with Cambridge came through his friendship with Dr Isaac Barrow, Master of Trinity and a

Trinity Library, the side to Nevile's Court with statues representing Divinity, Law, Physics and Mathematics.

great scholar both in mathematics and divinity. The first of two proposed buildings came to nothing. A drawing of a proposed Senate House shows a large building of three floors, and it is perhaps as well for Cambridge that money was not available for it. The second building is one of the finest in the University.

Wren took a great deal of trouble over the new library for Trinity College, and his first idea of a circular building with a dome was rejected. The plan eventually carried out closed Nevile's Court with an elegant building in Ketton stone, which has occasional pink blocks that give a pleasing warm glow. The rectangular library has very different fronts. The side facing the court has columns prominent at both levels, a wealth of carved capitals and other decoration. Centrally placed on the parapet are four statues representing Divinity, Law, Physics and Mathematics. The outer side is more austere with no ornament except for three doorways with Tuscan columns, and because there are no side ranges, the Library's superb proportions are better appreciated here.

Although the external columns indicate conventional storey heights, the floor of the Library is concealed behind the decorated panels at the top of the ground floor arches. Wren described his motives for doing this: he wanted to make the Library floor level with that in the side ranges and create a single compartment for the Library of sufficient height to accommodate windows above bookcases running continuously along the walls. Just as with Emmanuel chapel, Wren has used a Baroque device to reconcile the differences between inside and outside. The interior is magnificent. The bookcases by Cornelius Austin project to make bays for study and each has delicate carvings in lime wood by Grinling Gibbons. Trinity Library is thought to be the most personal of Wren's works. All the drawings exist in Wren's own exquisite hand and Robert Grumbold, the mason, travelled back and forth to London to see him.

The quality of Wren's three buildings came as a revelation to Cambridge. There had never before been buildings in which the conception was so perfect and in which craftsmen executed the details with such skill.

Trinity Library, the less ornate outer side. The floor level of the Library itself is just above the lower windows.

*Trinity Library undercroft. May
Ball celebrations and College
parties take place here.*

The Newtonian World

"The whole town is situate in a low dirty unpleasant place, the streets ill-paved, the air thick and infected by the fens." So wrote John Evelyn in 1654, well before Wren's great works, and he probably gave an accurate description of the town. Right up to the seventeenth century Cambridge was frequently visited by the plague and until comparatively recently there have been authenticated cases of students contracting illnesses from the watery surroundings. Evelyn was one of the first to record a visit to Cambridge. In 1697 Celia Fiennes admired Wren's library ("the finest carving in wood...as ever I saw") and Daniel Defoe in 1722 noted the unhealthy vapours arising from the fenland.

Defoe was however very impressed by Stourbridge Fair. This had begun on common land well to the east of the town at least by the early thirteenth century and had grown to the extent that five hundred years later it was (in Defoe's words) "not only the greatest in the whole nation but in the whole world". In September each year traders from all over Europe set up streets of booths, accompanied by taverns, eating places, brothels and all kinds of entertainments. Cloth Fair, Leather Fair, Ironmongers' Row, Horse Fair, Tallow Hill, Bookseller's Row and Oyster Fair were only a few of the areas set aside for various traders and commodities. Buyers and sightseers flocked to it from all over the country. Colleges bought stocks of provisions and candles. Coaches brought hundreds of visitors from London. The Mayor and Vice-Chancellor headed processions for the opening ceremony, which was followed by a banquet in the Oyster House. The University Proctors kept a watchful eye on the proceedings. It is likely that John Bunyan used Stourbridge Fair as the model for Vanity Fair in *Pilgrim's Progress* and scholars certainly bought books there. Isaac Newton is said to have bought his prism there. The Fair declined in the nineteenth century, and by the 1930's there were only a few booths. Today the only relic is a street called Garlic Row, off Newmarket Road.

In the eighteenth century river trade remained vital for the town in spite of difficulties arising from the drainage of the fens. Coal barges still came to Cambridge and where the riverside colleges refused to allow a towpath through their grounds a gravel path was laid in the middle of the river for horses to pull barges. The town remained very much subservient to the University, but tradesmen continued to make money from the increased wealth of the colleges.

There were now sixteen colleges, and although there was not much interest in the University from George I there was no interference from Government either. Cambridge became something of a backwater.

College eights train on the Cam beside Stourbridge Common, the site of Stourbridge Fair where goods from all over Europe were bought and sold for seven centuries.

Stage coaches ran regularly to several places, but it still took two days to reach London. Wealthy fellow commoners and pensioners attracted the most attention, but the majority of Cambridge students were not well off and some were very poor indeed. By hard work they could raise their position, and for many their highest ambitions were to obtain a church "living" as vicar or rector.

From the Restoration the natural sciences began to play a larger part in Cambridge learning. In 1664 the Lucasian Professorship of Mathematics was founded, and the first professor was Isaac Barrow, later Master of Trinity College. Mathematics came to be the most important subject studied and this was largely due to Barrow and to Barrow's greatest pupil, Isaac Newton.

Newton entered Trinity in 1660 and became a Fellow seven years later. He was soon drawn to scientific experiments and his progress was so remarkable that Barrow resigned and made Newton Professor of Mathematics at the age of twenty-six. Altogether Newton resided in Cambridge for thirty-five years. He discovered the binomial theorem and the differential calculus, and carried out experiments on the nature of light, using a prism which is illustrated in the moving statue of Newton by Roubiliac in the college Antechapel. His great work *Principia Mathematica* (written in Latin for its international audience), was published in 1687 but is the result of work done over a long period. It embodies his laws on motion and gravity. Cambridge did not realise the full significance of Newton's work for a long time, but his greatness was apparent, and his influence on Cambridge thought was incalculable. He was knighted by Queen Anne in the Master's Lodge at Trinity, but he spent the last thirty years of his life in London, and for most of them he was annually re-elected as President of the Royal Society. Newton was undoubtedly the greatest genius the University has produced and *Principia Mathematica* the most important scientific work ever published. Isaac Barrow during his period as Master had enabled Newton to realise his genius and Wren to build a masterpiece.

One other scholar should be mentioned, Richard Bentley, originally a sizar of St John's, appointed Master of Trinity in 1700, a post he retained for over forty years. He was the greatest theologian of his day, and the greatest classical scholar England has produced. When appointed Master, Bentley had just won a famous victory over Oxford on the classical writer Phalaris and proved as fearless an administrator as he had been scholar. He made much-needed changes in Trinity and promoted the development of Natural Sciences by providing a laboratory for the newly-founded Professor of Chemistry and an observatory on top of the Great Gate (later removed) for the first Plumian Professor of Astronomy. But he is unfortunately best remembered for the way he exploited and hung on to the Mastership, against powerful opposition, through a combination of good luck, determination and ruthlessness.

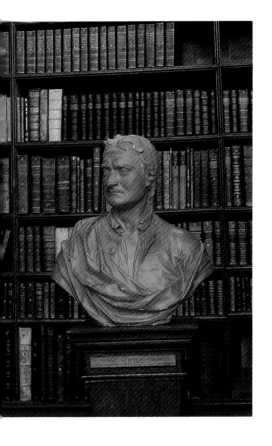

Terracotta bust of Sir Isaac Newton by Rysbrack in Trinity Library.

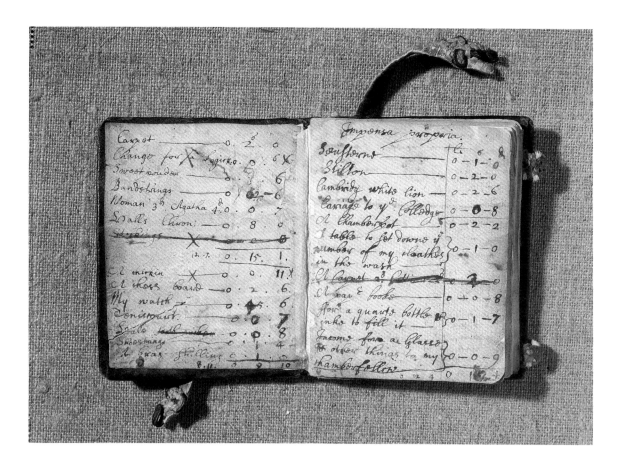

Newton's pocket book, on display in Trinity Library, in which he recorded his expenses on everyday needs such as ink and washing.

Apart from these men and a very few others, Cambridge was not notable for scholarship in the eighteenth century. College life took precedence over the University and each college went its individual way. Discipline was slack, Fellows neglected their duties and only the most assiduous of students achieved much in the way of learning, and then usually through private tutors. Fellows were still not allowed to retain their Fellowship on marriage, and so their choice was between married life in a rectory (if they could find one) or a celibate existence in college.

College tutors performed what teaching there was and the University professors were not called upon to do very much. The story of Richard Watson bears this out. He began as a sizar, became a respected mathematician and later a Fellow of Trinity. In 1764 he was made Professor of Chemistry when "he had never read a syllable on the subject nor seen a single experiment in it", but in time apparently became competent. Seven years later, having never studied theology, he was appointed Regius Professor of Divinity. Later still he became Bishop of Llandaff but it is no surprise that he should prefer to go on living in Cambridge.

This kind of life suited those who wanted leisure to pursue some kind of intellectual work without undue pressure. One such person was Thomas Gray who entered Peterhouse as a fellow commoner in 1734 and, apart

Roubiliac's bust of Richard Bentley, Master of Trinity for over forty years, in Trinity Library with Grinling Gibbons' carving above.

from a few years travelling with Horace Walpole, never again left Cambridge. Grey wrote a small amount of poetry, the most famous being the *Elegy Written in a Country Churchyard*.

Being afraid that fire could be started by drunken undergraduates, Grey installed a fire escape from his room in the newly built Burrough's building. The iron bar from which he hung his rope ladder can still be seen. One morning in 1746 his neighbours aroused him with a false alarm. So Gray decided that he would be better off elsewhere and went across Trumpington Street to Pembroke. He eventually became Professor of History but never wrote the large work he contemplated.

Another poet at Pembroke, Christopher Smart, gained a reputation as a brilliant scholar and poet, but after taking his degree he drank heavily, got into debt and eventually died insane in a debtors' prison. He left some witty lyrics and two fine poems, *A Song to David* and *Jubilate Agno*, that reveal his curious imagination.

In the middle of the century Laurence Sterne was at Jesus, benefitting from a scholarship funded by his great-grandfather, a former Master of Jesus and Archbishop of York. Sterne became famous as author of *Tristram Shandy* which contains some sharply drawn caricatures of academics that reflect the low opinion widespread in his day.

Towards the end of the century the town entered a period when corruption and inefficiency were paramount. The Council and town Members of Parliament were elected by the freemen, who were not much

Jesus College Library dating from 1665-75, as Laurence Sterne, author of Tristram Shandy, *might have used it when an undergraduate.*

The Library Court, Trinity Hall, right, showing both Tudor brickwork and the refacing by Burrough in the eighteenth century.

more than a hundred in number and who did not all live in the town. From the 1780's the town came under the domination of John Mortlock who was very wealthy through his father's drapery business and his own marriage. Mortlock became a freeman at the age of twenty-three, a councillor and then Mayor at thirty-two, in 1787. In the next quarter of a century he was Mayor thirteen times, every other year, and in the intervening years one of his sons or business associates took his place. Town property was sold cheaply to his friends, charitable funds disappeared, and Mortlock's supporters did virtually what they liked. But there were attempts to improve the paving, cleaning and lighting of Cambridge. Mortlock, incidentally, opened the first bank in Cambridge, at his town house in Bene't Street, where the house of the Austin Friars had once been.

A Muted Classicism

The dormant state of Cambridge in the eighteenth century is reflected in its buildings, for Cambridge had very little good original work after Wren, unlike Oxford. The major rebuilding of Clare, begun in 1638, and of St Catharine's, begun in 1674, was largely complete by the end of the seventeenth century. Work on the west and north ranges of Clare was continued after the Restoration, making the Old Court the first completely classical court in the University. The influence of Wren is clearly seen in the great Ionic order of the west front facing the river, and in the severe dignity of the north range, which contains the hall. This is not surprising as Wren's chapels at Pembroke and Emmanuel were much admired and the builder of Clare was Robert Grumbold, who worked with Wren on Trinity Library and was probably responsible for the tribune or rostrum which balances the Library across Nevile's Court.

The West Range of Clare, below, and the Old Bridge at St John's, below right, both built by Grumbold.

Grumbold came from a Northamptonshire family of masons and he has left his mark on Cambridge in several places. In addition to Clare, Grumbold was responsible for the rebuilding of St Catharine's which had been founded on a small scale in the late fifteenth century by Robert Woodlarke, Provost of King's. David Loggan's print shows that the new building was to have been a four-sided court with the entrance in Queens' Lane. Grumbold's work is good, if unexciting, the best part being the chapel, quite clearly based on Wren and built with the advice of William Talman. He used brick, with dressings of stone, which would no doubt have been cheaper than the stone of Clare.

Grumbold also built one of the most attractive bridges across the Cam, that of St John's, based on suggestions from Wren. His father Thomas Grumbold had built the oldest surviving bridge at Clare nearly seventy years previously. Both are extremely elegant, with balustrades and carved panels, those at St John's containing a representation of the god of the river. It is good to record that Robert Grumbold is remembered in a simple tablet on the outer wall of St Botolph's church.

In 1713 Nicholas Hawksmoor was asked to produce a plan for completing King's College, of which only the chapel had been built, with the remainder of the college carrying on in crowded quarters behind Old Schools. Hawksmoor's plan had a monumental gateway, great hall, a cloister with a tall bell tower and a small court with the Provost's Lodge. This and even a modified plan were rejected by the college as too grand. Hawksmoor went further and produced a plan for the centre of Cambridge in which the main feature was to be a broad avenue stretching along Petty Cury from Christ's College to the east end of King's Chapel, where there was to be a forum with colonnades. Trinity Street was to be widened and straightened, with obelisks as focal points, and a further street made from Trinity Great Gate to Sidney Sussex College. The plan would have made a splendid University area in the town centre, with noble classical buildings and fine vistas. But nobody was interested. Apart from the financial aspect, it was not as easy then to clear away citizen's houses and shops, as Henry VI had found three centuries before.

King's got part of its Great Court ten years later. James Gibbs (who had been working on London churches, including St Clement Danes and St Martin-in-the-Fields) produced a modified version of Hawksmoor's Fellows Building, with much less decoration, though with a grand archway in axis with the gate (which was not yet built) and the bridge over the river. It is in Portland stone and still has a number of Baroque features. Gibbs also designed the best eighteenth century building in Cambridge, the Senate House.

The Sheldonian Theatre had provided Oxford with a building for University ceremonies for over fifty years. In 1722 Gibbs proposed a court with a library in front of the Old Schools, a Senate House on one side and a matching building for University offices on the other, with Great St Mary making the fourth side. Only the Senate House was built, in Portland stone and with a number of Palladian features. It is a noble building, with pilasters on either side of the three central bays which are brought forward with columns supporting a graceful pediment. Inside is one long room with narrow galleries on three sides.

The Senate House is all the better for not having anything facing it. But it gains from its neighbour, the Palladian building erected by Stephen Wright thirty years later to house the University library. The University had acquired books slowly until 1715 when George I was persuaded to buy the library of John Moore, Bishop of Ely, and present it to the University. Wright's elegant five-bay building, with cloister underneath, contained the King's Library until a larger one was needed over eighty years later.

The most typical architects working in Cambridge were Sir James Burrough and James Essex. Burrough was an amateur architect (as many were at this time, including Lord Burlington) and later became Master of Gonville and Caius. He designed one fine building, the Palladian block

at Peterhouse, but is also remembered for the first refacing of a college court. Mediaeval buildings were regarded as inferior and inartistic. Several colleges wanted more modern courts but were reluctant or unable to pay for new buildings. Burrough refaced the principal court of Trinity Hall with a thin coat of ashlar, included a pediment, and inserted sash windows. On entering the court the impression is of a classical court, but the illusion is quickly dispelled by a look at the backs of the ranges, where it is easy to see the fourteenth century rubble, with later brick repairs, and some of the original windows.

James Essex was younger and more professional. He worked occasionally with Horace Walpole and took an interest in Gothic architecture, though his surviving work in Cambridge is all in classical style. At one time or another he worked on the majority of Cambridge's

colleges, a number of which he refaced in stone, including First Court of Christ's (which was given a Venetian window inside the Gate Tower) and one side of First Court of St John's – fortunately the college could afford no more.

Essex built residential blocks in the Palladian style at Queens' and St Catharine's. He remodelled the cloisters in Trinity's Nevile's Court and he designed the elegant entrance for Emmanuel. Essex redesigned the hall at Emmanuel providing panelling and concealing the fine hammer-beam roof with a beautiful plaster ceiling. In keeping with the current dislike of mediaeval styles, many college halls and chapels received similar treatment though, unlike Emmanuel's hall, further changes have restored the original form.

Some halls became more like rooms in large mansions, to suit the taste for greater luxury. The smaller college chapels became more suitable for services of which the most important feature was the sermon. In Great St Mary extra galleries were inserted, one at the west end in front of the tower, another, almost unbelievably, across the chancel, where Doctors and Heads of Colleges sat with their backs to the altar. With the two existing side galleries the preacher was surrounded by an audience on all sides.

Classical architecture, domestic and collegiate. Little Trinity, 1725, above, and the entrance to Emmanuel by James Essex, 1769.

There was no shortage of eminent architects eager to build in Cambridge. In 1784 Robert Adam, at the height of his fame and with successful buildings at Edinburgh University behind him, made an attempt to complete the Great Court of King's (his plans included a circular hall), but it proved unacceptable to the College. He also prepared designs for a new University Library, but they were too ambitious and so Adam left no mark on Cambridge.

Even more exciting would have been the landscaping of the Backs which Capability Brown had proposed a few years earlier. This would have treated the Backs as a whole instead of dividing the river up into separate college areas and would have created a beautiful riverside walk. Predictably the colleges concerned could not agree. It is tantalising to imagine what Cambridge would have been like had Hawksmoor's plans been carried out, with additional buildings by Robert Adam and a landscaped river. It would certainly have been a different Cambridge, but something of the intimacy of the present haphazard merging of town and University would have been destroyed.

James Wyatt was a third famous architect to have plans turned down, for the new Downing College in 1784 and for King's ten years later, both were in the revived Gothic style. Wyatt was a little ahead of Cambridge taste, for the style was to become very acceptable before long.

Chapter 6

Town sites
University sites

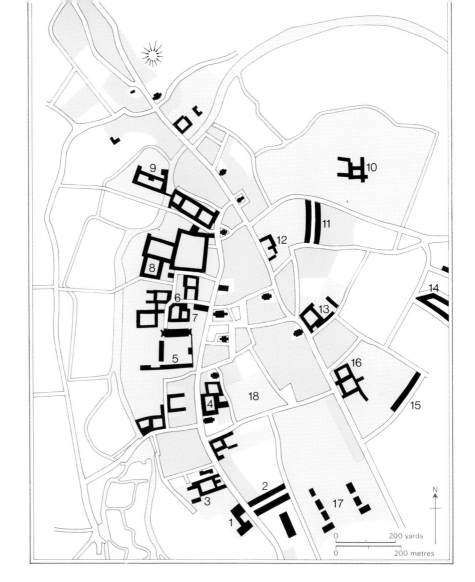

The view from a punt: the Bridge of Sighs at St John's in spring.

The Ubiquitous Wilkins

The strangest story of all Cambridge college foundations is that of Downing, which took place over fifty years after the death of its founder. The Downing family's fortunes came with the first Baronet, Sir George Downing, who was one of the first graduates of Harvard College in Massachusetts, had various careers in New England and in Cromwell's England, changed sides at the Restoration and was involved in several lucrative enterprises including speculative building (among which was Downing Street in London). Pepys referred to him as a "perfidious rogue". His grandson, also Sir George, lived at Gamlingay, apart from his wife, and drew up a will stipulating that his estates were to pass in turn to four cousins. If they died without children the money was to be used to found a college called after him in Cambridge. In 1764 when the last cousin, Sir Jacob Downing, died without an heir the college should have been founded. But Sir Jacob's widow refused to give up the estates and a series of costly lawsuits dragged on for thirty years. In a final act of spite she burnt down the Gamlingay house. Eventually in 1800 Downing College received its charter.

*Downing College: the great court
defined by classical forms.*

It was over two hundred years since the last Cambridge college, Sidney Sussex, had been founded in 1596 and the new college was to have certain innovations. King George III insisted that the buildings were to be classical in style, only two Fellows had to be in holy orders and there were to be two new Downing Professors of Medicine and Law, each with a house on the college site. The first Professor of Law was Edward Christian, brother of Fletcher Christian of the Bounty mutiny. James Essex and James Wyatt had prepared plans before 1800, but the architect chosen was William Wilkins, a Fellow of Gonville and Caius, who produced a classical design derived from buildings he had seen on visits to Greece. On a large site well to the south of the town there was to be a very large court, larger than Trinity's Great Court, with three detached mansions and Master's Lodge on the east facing three more mansions and hall on the west. The south side was to contain a grand chapel and library, and the north a monumental entrance, approached from the town by an avenue. The buildings were to have columns with Ionic capitals and pediments, making a magnificent classical ensemble on a grand scale.

Even then there were difficulties acquiring the land and collecting enough money not only to build the college but pay the stipends of the Fellows. The foundation stone was laid by the Master, Francis Annesley, and building started in 1807. Building proceeded slowly; the Master's Lodge was completed in 1811 but the Master never moved in and died in London in 1812. The remainder of the east and west ranges were completed by 1821 when the first undergraduates came up. Further work on the east and west ranges was done in the 1870's. The northern part of the site was sold to the University in 1906, so the avenue and entrance were never built. A modified version of the northern range was completed in the 1950's. Little remained of Wilkins' grand design except the Grecian qualities of the original buildings.

After the Napoleonic Wars there was an increase in the number of students attending the University and several colleges could not contain them without further building. Extra ranges were put up at Peterhouse, Jesus, Emmanuel and Christ's, and all of them were very dull. All are of brick and had imitation Gothic windows and battlements but in three of them the brickwork was covered with cement. The horror of Roman cement can be seen most clearly at Sidney Sussex, which had no additions at the time but which for some strange reason allowed Sir Jeffry Wyatville to cover up the warm red Elizabethan brick and to add battlements and crow-stepped gables. By the 1820's mediaeval styles had become fashionable, especially in colleges now very conscious of their antiquity.

But in four colleges there was better work, which was fortunate as the new buildings were in prominent places. Three of them were by William Wilkins, who was also responsible for the National Gallery and University College, London. When asked for designs for a new court at Trinity, Wilkins produced two, one classical and one Gothic. The college chose the latter, and so New Court contains plenty of mediaeval features: gate tower, embattled parapets, Gothic windows, heraldry and even niches for statues. The main material is brick but it was covered in Roman cement.

Gothic Revival by Wilkins at Corpus Christi, under the gatehouse with the chapel behind.

For Corpus Christi's new court Wilkins produced a complete court in the mediaeval manner entered through a gate tower with new hall, chapel, library and Master's Lodge. Its erection involved the destruction of the Elizabethan chapel and a corner of the Old Court which became little more than a picturesque appendage. The former hall was relegated to become the new kitchens. New Court is a beautiful composition and was Wilkins' own favourite in his Gothic style. The gate tower is vaulted above the entrance and directly faces the chapel where Wilkins is buried. To left and right are the great hall and the library, the latter particularly impressive because it was to contain Archbishop Parker's wonderful collection of manuscripts. The whole court is faced with Ketton stone and has battlements all round. Its outer facade adds balance and dignity to Trumpington Street.

In 1823 King's College at last decided to complete the Great Court that their founder had begun nearly four centuries before. Wilkins won the competition to complete the remaining two sides. The Chapel was, as it is now, widely regarded as the finest building in Cambridge and among the finest in the whole country. Wilkins decided to build a screen on the front of the court with large Perpendicular windows and pinnacles to

echo some of the Chapel's most striking features. In the centre the gate tower has a cluster of loftier pinnacles with a prominent cupola. It all adds up to an original fantasy on Gothic themes, liberally adorned with Tudor roses, crowns and portcullises. Clearing away the houses in front of the screen opened up fine views of the Chapel and created one of the best loved of all Cambridge townscapes.

For the side of the court facing the Chapel, Wilkins designed the hall, which has perpendicular windows, battlements and more Tudor emblems, but also a centrally-placed bay window and two lanterns in the roof, making it the most unusual and un-Gothic of all mediaeval-style halls. These features contribute to the symmetry of this side of the court, just as the other three sides are symmetrical. It was no small achievement on Wilkins' part to complete so satisfactorily a Great Court that already had fifteenth and eighteenth century buildings in very different styles.

One of Cambridge's famous views was created in the 1820's when St John's College decided to build New Court across the river, the first of the colleges to do so. Rickman and Hutchinson built a large three-sided court closed on the south by a screen with a gateway and cloister walk. (Thomas Rickman was the man who gave the names Early English, Decorated and Perpendicular to the phases of English Gothic.) It is a large building of four storeys, with a squat central tower crowned with a prominent lantern with flying buttresses and pinnacles. This lantern and the screen save New Court from being yet another mediocre residence block. Seen from the Backs across the lawn the skyline of New Court is exciting and romantic. The court was linked to the older part of the college by the Bridge of Sighs, the Gothic windows of which have bars to prevent illicit access.

The University also found it necessary to expand. Although the colleges all had libraries, some of them important, the University had also acquired a library of its own, chiefly through donations, the largest coming from George I in 1715. By the turn of the century there was a serious lack of space, and in 1837 a new library building was commissioned. C. R. Cockerell was chosen as architect and he produced a building in a Grecian style next to the Old Divinity School. As so often happened in Cambridge only one range of a much larger library court was built, which accounts for the curious overlapping with the Old Schools. It is difficult to get a good view of the library as a whole, but it has a European style of some architectural interest. It is still a law library but no longer the University library.

In 1816 Viscount Fitzwilliam bequeathed a collection of paintings, prints, manuscripts and books, with investment income to house the collection and to purchase further works of art. After delays in selecting a site, George Basevi produced the winning design, a heavy classical building with large Corinthian capitals. It was begun in 1837, some galleries were ready for part of the collection in 1848, but the museum had not been completed when Basevi fell to his death at Ely Cathedral three years later. It was completed in the 1870's by E. M. Barry. Alongside the Gothic Revival other styles were still used, and classical forms were considered particularly appropriate for libraries, museums and public buildings.

A collection for a statue of Pitt the Younger was held in the early 1800's. It yielded sufficient money not only to provide the statue which stands in the gardens of Pembroke, his old college, but also to build the Pitt Building in Trumpington Street for the University Press.

In 1801 the population of Cambridge was not much over nine thousand and the town was still crowded into more or less the same area as in the Middle Ages. Here too change was necessary and Enclosure Acts of 1802

King's College Hall, a Gothic fantasy roof line by Wilkins.

and 1807 provided space for expansion to east and west. Estates and speculative building appeared, much of it routine. But there were exceptions. There are good town terraces, for example, Fitzwilliam Street and Malcolm Street. New Square is an almost complete early nineteenth century square, all the better for having its centre recently returned to grass. Not far away, Orchard Street is an attractive terrace of small cottages. The grandest of all Cambridge town housing, Park Terrace, overlooking Parker's Piece, is three-storey housing with fine wrought iron balconies.

In 1815, before the wave of University building of the 1820's, Rudolf Ackermann's artists visited Cambridge to make drawings for his collection of prints. They show a town still mediaeval in many ways. The expansion of town and University began shortly afterwards.

Rickman's Gothic Revival cloister of New Court, St John's, and one of the carved heads that decorate the gateway.

New Court, St John's, seen from the spacious lawns of Trinity.

Romanticism and Poets

Despite the shortcomings of the education provided at the time, numbers at the University grew, including an impressive cross-section of men later to become famous as writers. Their reactions to Cambridge are interesting. William Wordsworth was fresh from the mountains and lakes of Westmorland. His autobiographical poem, *The Prelude*, gives a lively account of his early days at St John's, the excitement of his new life and his sense of wonder at being where great figures of the past had been. Wordsworth was a sizar, and even his small bare room above the kitchen could not spoil his enjoyment.

It was not long before he became disillusioned by the highly competitive mathematics, compulsory daily chapel services, and the idleness and vices of many of his fellows, "I was not for that hour, Nor for that place". Wordsworth became a "non-reading man", and his most profitable experiences came from walks in the Cambridgeshire fields and in his vacations. On the other hand his younger brother Christopher applied himself hard to his studies, did well, and eventually became Master of his college, Trinity.

Front entrance to the Fitzwilliam Museum in Trumpington Street.

Samuel Taylor Coleridge, who arrived at Jesus shortly after Wordsworth departed from St John's, was more extrovert and acquired a reputation for brilliance. But he also began taking opium and got into debt. His interests became capricious: he took up revolutionary politics and Unitarianism, he wrote poetry, discussed the latest pamphlets. In his final year Coleridge had a minor breakdown and disappeared, to enlist as a dragoon. He was an incompetent horseman, and after four months, when his friends had traced him, his officers were relieved to discharge him as "insane". In his last vacation Coleridge met Robert Southey at Oxford, and together they devised "pantisocracy", a scheme for setting up a society in America where wealth and work would be shared equally. Back in Cambridge, Coleridge printed a verse play which he and Southey had written, *The Fall of Robespierre*, which caused a minor scandal among the University authorities. At the same time other literary enterprises failed to materialise and he was involved with three women. Coleridge fled to London and did not return.

Wordsworth received scarcely any encouragement but Coleridge was constantly helped by Jesus College and his friends. The revolutionary ardour which had affected many students including both Wordsworth and Coleridge had been subdued by the excesses of the Terror and the war with France but the colleges had not changed when Byron arrived. Trevelyan in his historical sketch of Trinity College says "In 1805 Byron came up from Harrow to Trinity. He was, as his tutor noted, a youth of tumultuous passions. As a nobleman he was scarcely expected to take much interest in the studies of the place and he did not. He lived very

94

One of the milestones around Cambridge set up in 1725 by Dr Warren of Trinity Hall. Measurements were made from a stone in the tower of Great St Mary's.

fast. To mention his more innocent pleasures, he was writing his early satires and poems, riding, shooting with pistols and boxing. The weir above Grantchester is called Byron's Pool because he swam there; he also swam matches in the Thames under the training of his friend Jackson, the pugilist, who had more influence on him than his official Tutor, the excellent Thomas Jones. Byron, observing that there was a statute against keeping dogs in College but none against keeping bears, lodged a bear in the top attic of the tower at the south-east corner of Great Court, then called Mutton-hole corner. He took Bruin for walks on a chain like a dog, and said he should sit for a Fellowship, and teach the Fellows manners."

Byron took his M.A. degree in 1808, a formality for a nobleman. When he returned to Cambridge six years later he was famous as the author of *Childe Harold's Pilgrimage* and received a rapturous reception in the Senate House. It is a credit to his college that the fine statue by the Danish sculptor Thorwaldsen, rejected by Westminster Abbey because of the poet's morals, now has a place of honour in Trinity Library.

At Cambridge walking and riding were the traditional means of taking exercise, but by the 1820's organised games were gaining in popularity. Cricket had been played on a small scale by undergraduates who came from the great public schools as early as the eighteenth century. About 1825 a University Cricket Club was founded, and in 1846 it moved to fields rented from Mr F. P. Fenner, a town cricketer. The first Oxford and Cambridge match was played in 1827.

Rowing had a similar beginning in the public schools and men from Trinity and St John's began races in the mid-1820's. The narrowness of the river made bumping races more practical, and races of up to ten boats were recorded from 1828. The next year a challenge was delivered to Oxford and the first Boat Race was held at Henley-on-Thames, when Oxford, wearing dark blue jerseys, were the winners. In 1836 Cambridge decorated their boat with light blue ribbon.

Intercollegiate activities also had a more intellectual side. In 1815 the Union Society was formed for public debates and although it was soon closed by the authorities, it reappeared in 1821 with the proviso that contemporary politics were not discussed. It quickly assumed the popularity it has continued to hold to the present day. In 1820 the Cambridge Conversazione Society was formed at St John's, a small elite circle of men chosen by invitation and better known as "The Apostles". Both the Union and the exclusive Apostles attracted the leading intellectuals of the day. Many important writers and philosophers of the nineteenth century were members of one or both including Macaulay, Tennyson and Thackeray.

Macaulay came up to Trinity in 1818 and resided in the same staircase as Newton. He worked hard, read widely and carried off a number of university prizes, but like so many more he was unable to succeed in

Essex versus the University at Fenner's Lawn. The spire of the Roman Catholic Church built in the late nineteenth century can be seen.

mathematics and so did not take an honours degree, which would have ensured an academic career. Trinity, however, thought sufficiently highly of him to elect him a Fellow. For some time Macaulay dominated the Union before going on to a great career in politics and to write his *History of England*. When Trinity came to make a decision on the statues to be placed in their antechapel, Macauley was consulted and supported the suggestion of Bentley, whom he said had established the pattern of Cambridge scholarship. However, dislike of Bentley was still strong enough to ensure that Barrow was chosen instead.

Thackeray's stay in Cambridge was not unlike that of the hero in his novel *Pendennis*. He read and worked, not sufficiently to succeed in examinations, but enough to make a reputation writing for undergraduate magazines. He made friends, and drank and gambled his way into debt. Thackeray gave us the modern word "snob". In Cambridge "snob" had been the slang word for a townsman, but Thackeray, in the *Book of Snobs* widened this to include anyone who makes himself ridiculous or unpleasant by the value set on social standing.

The strangest of all Trinity writers in the 1820's was Alfred Tennyson, who arrived from a lonely and odd upbringing in the Lincolnshire wolds and was instantly recognisable as a poet in the Byronic tradition. He smoked a pipe for most of the day and visited places associated with Milton, Byron and other great men. Despite his contempt for the University and its teaching, he was fond of Cambridge. So he read, wrote poetry (winning the Chancellor's Medal in 1829) and in his second year made friends with Arthur Hallam, whose untimely death a few years later inspired the moving tribute *In Memoriam*.

The system of teaching during the past hundred and fifty years was now quite inadequate. In 1824 the Classics Tripos provided an alternative path to an honours degree, but change was very slow to come. The bias towards mathematics continued, most Fellows were still in holy orders, there was little instruction in the natural sciences, the religious Test Acts still applied, it was becoming increasingly difficult for all but the wealthy to attend, and of course there were no women students.

Early in the century a Patrick Brunty graduated at St John's. He changed his name afterwards to the more respectable-sounding "Bronte". He was the father of three remarkable and intelligent daughters for whom there was no possibility whatever of a university education.

Following the college boats in the bumps, May Week. Supporters of the eights wear pass tickets to allow them to cycle on the towpath during the races.

Prince Albert and Reforms

Towards the end of 1843, Queen Victoria and Prince Albert made their first visit to Cambridge, escorted for the last few miles by a large body of yeomanry and greeted at a triumphal arch in Trumpington Street by the Mayor and Town Council. The Queen drove into Trinity Great Court, where the University dignitaries and a large body of dons and students awaited her, and the usual loyal addresses were presented. The Queen and Prince Consort attended evensong in King's College Chapel and afterwards visited Trinity Chapel, to see Newton's statue. Next day Prince Albert received an Honorary Degree in the Senate House, and there were further visits to colleges. It was a much more formal occasion than the visit of Queen Elizabeth two and a half centuries earlier, but possibly its consequences were more important.

Four years later the couple returned, this time by train as the railway had now reached Cambridge. With another round of receptions, concerts and ceremonies, Prince Albert was installed as Chancellor in the Senate

Seventeenth century houses opposite the Fitzwilliam Museum.

A row of town houses in Little St Mary's Lane dating from the sixteenth to the nineteenth century.

House. The appointment was significant, because the Prince Consort was well aware of the need for change in the University. He knew what was happening in universities on the Continent, and was anxious for Cambridge University to take its place in the modern world, if possible without outside interference. He asked the Vice-Chancellor to provide him with information about "the scheme of tuition in the colleges separately and the University for the ensuing year". He wanted to know the subjects taught and examined, the authors to be read and the lectures to be given by the various professors. The Prince cannot have been impressed by what he heard. He wanted more subjects taught and in 1848 Natural Sciences and Moral Sciences were added.

This was not the first time that reform had been mentioned. In 1837 an MP for Cambridge had proposed in the House of Commons that a Commission be appointed to look into the state of the universities. The motion was defeated and a counter petition was presented to the House of Lords, signed by resident graduates and undergraduates, begging that no changes be made to the University's statutes.

In 1850 a Royal Commission was appointed to examine the efficiency of the universities, and eight years later the Cambridge University Act made important changes. Commissioners were appointed to revise University and college statutes, Boards of Studies controlled the subjects taught, restrictions on elections to fellowships and scholarships were removed and, most important, the University regained its supervision of the colleges, who would now be required to contribute more to University funds. The authority of the colleges was over.

The term "Tripos" dates from the fifteenth century and is still used in Cambridge for honours examinations. It comes from the three-legged stool on which a bachelor sat, in the presence of the Proctors, to question and argue with the candidate. These disputations, an essential part of the mediaeval system, continued until well into the nineteenth century. From about 1770 there were written examinations. The Law Tripos was set up in 1858, the History Tripos in 1872 and the Theology Tripos two years later. The University was beginning to take its modern form. The quality of the new professors and lecturers appointed showed that higher standards were being set.

Another reform deprived King's College of rights it had had since its foundation. The College had been placed by its founder outside the jurisdiction of the Bishop of Ely and the University Chancellor, and King's undergraduates could take a degree without a University examination. From 1851 this anomaly was ended.

The number of wealthy young men in residence made it hard for any except those with substantial means to live in a college. So in 1869 the University set up the Non-Collegiate Student Board by which students could follow a degree course without being resident in a college. They lived in lodgings, attended lectures, used libraries and took degrees in the ordinary way. They lived much the kind of life that was usual in the early days of the University. The Board acquired a fine eighteenth century brick mansion in Trumpington Street. This was named Fitzwilliam Hall (later Fitzwilliam House) as it was opposite the museum. After the Second World War when government grants to students rendered it unnecessary, Fitzwilliam House became Fitzwilliam College.

Two further reforms were necessary to bring the University out of the Middle Ages. Until 1871 no Dissenter could become an M.A. or a college Fellow. All had to be members of the Church of England, subscribe to the Thirty-nine Articles, and attend four to eight services a week in the college chapel regularly. In the 1830's the House of Commons had passed a Bill to change this, but it had been thrown out by the House of Lords. In 1871 the religious Test Acts were finally abolished.

The second legacy of the mediaeval past was the ban against the marriage of Fellows. If a Fellow remained unmarried he could look forward to a secure life in college whether he taught or not. If, as was usual, the Fellow was in holy orders, and he married, he might expect one of the church livings in the gift of the college. In 1882 this was changed. A Fellow was permitted to marry and a life fellowship was associated with a post in the college or University.

These reforms gave the University a clearer sense of direction and purpose. They reflected changes taking place in the country where necessary reforms were being carried out to meet the needs of an expanding population in a society rapidly becoming industrialised. Living conditions for a large numbers of people were appalling, but a social conscience was being awakened.

Cambridge shared in these national trends. The population of the town increased four-fold during the century, rather more if outlying villages were included. In the mid-century about a sixth of the population of Cambridge lived in houses tucked away in courts without drainage or water supply. The small settlement of Barnwell, where the old Augustinian Priory had been, had no more than two hundred inhabitants in 1800. Sixty years later there were thirteen thousand, and overcrowding, squalor and malnutrition, and consequently crime and prostitution, were rife. The Bishop of Ely referred to Barnwell as "a dark spot, close to the very focus of light". There were other dark spots, including the former inn-yards off Petty Cury, right in the heart of the town. Philanthropists from colleges and town set up missions to try to help.

Corruption in town management grew less when Mortlock and his friends lost control. The climate was changing. The University no longer insisted on its rights and submitted to arbitration over disputes with the town. The Cambridge Award Act of 1856 made some important changes. The Mayor and Council no longer had to swear to maintain the rights and privileges of the University. The town could now control its

The Eagle Yard today. The open gallery gives access to rooms above. The ceiling of the main bar preserves the signatures of Second World War pilots who flew from airbases in East Anglia.

The Avenue at the back of Trinity College with fine wrought iron gates containing the college arms given by Henry Bromley in 1733.

own markets and fairs, supervise weights and measures, and licence ale-houses. Above all, the right of "conusance" was withdrawn, which meant that civil or criminal law cases in which a member of the University was a party could no longer be tried in a University Court. But the University retained the right to prohibit certain entertainments and was strongly represented on the Council. The Proctors, too, retained their powers, one of which was the right to arrest women thought to be prostitutes. The Vice-Chancellor could commit them to the Spinning House, which had once been a House of Correction. The University only gave up this right in 1894.

All these changes took place within not much more than a quarter of a century from Prince Albert's installation as Chancellor and his vision and enthusiasm must have helped. The University was now attracting many more students, and this in turn led to further changes.

Chapter 7

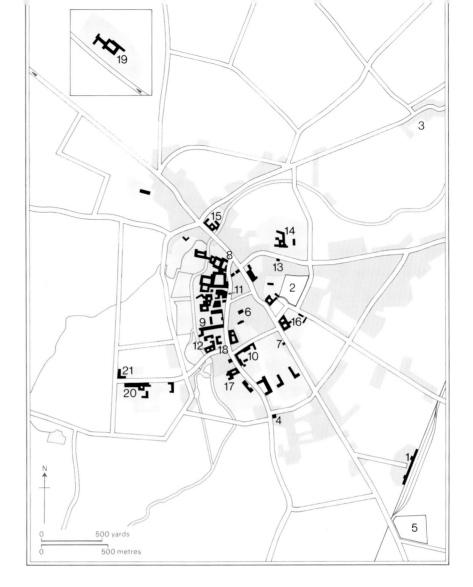

Town sites
University sites

The view northwards from Great St Mary's tower. In the foreground, Gonville and Caius, beside Trinity Street which leads to Trinity and St John's.

The Railway and Urban Expansion

The town of Cambridge began to assume its modern shape in the second half of the nineteenth century. The most important factor was the coming of the railway in 1845, after twenty years of proposals and abortive schemes. Plans for a railway station close to the town centre were quickly thwarted by college heads. But the University authorities were unable to prohibit the railway altogether, though they compelled the company to build the station at a considerable distance from the town in open country. In the Act enabling the Eastern Counties Railway Company to build the line the University managed to get clauses inserted giving University officers the power of access to platforms and demand information about persons thought to be members of the University. The Company could be fined for carrying students, even if a fare had been paid, and was also prohibited from picking up or setting down passengers within three miles of Cambridge station between 10 am and 3 pm on Sundays. Not long afterwards cheap day return tickets on an early Sunday train were issued, causing the Vice-Chancellor to protest

The railway station, recently modernised when the line was electrified. The medallions are the arms of Cambridge colleges.

that Sunday excursions were "as distasteful to the University authorities as they must be offensive to Almighty God and to all right minded Christians". The Sunday train restrictions were not repealed until 1908, though they had not been invoked for some time before then.

The Great Northern Railway wanted a second line to Cambridge and a station near Christ's Pieces, a proposal supported by the Town Council but vigorously opposed by the Master of Christ's who said it would "render Christ's and Emmanuel Colleges almost uninhabitable". At last, in 1866, the Great Northern Railway (the present King's Cross line) reached Cambridge, using part of the existing station. Cambridge station is one of the few remaining with a cross-over and a single platform which is twice as long as a train. This is echoed on the street side where the architect, Sancton Wood, has created an elegant arcade of fifteen arches in an Italianate style.

The railway had immediate consequences for Cambridge. It marked the end of stage coach travel (though it is pleasant to learn that the driver of the last coach obtained employment with the railway) and a gradual decline in river traffic, though river and rail continued jointly for some time to come. Rows of terrace houses for railway workers were built on the east side of the town. The open fields disappeared and the station was no longer isolated. Expansion took place to the north-east as well and the old village of Chesterton gradually merged with Cambridge.

Most of the west side was unusable for building before the river was controlled by locks and drainage. The scenery of the Backs was preserved and a large area beyond was free for subsequent development. This area began to be built on during the last quarter of the nineteenth century, partly for Fellows' houses. The newly-gained freedom of Fellows to marry enabled them to build substantial houses with large gardens suitable for raising families. Such houses required servants for their upkeep, but there was no problem in finding these from the large numbers now overcrowding the town.

Changes in the town came automatically with the enormous and continuing rise in population, and the autonomy slowly gained from the University. Churches and schools were being built in the new suburbs, and the council took a more active role in the welfare and planning of the town from 1849 when a fire destroyed houses and shops in Market Hill. The Council decided not to rebuild them but enlarge the market to the size and shape it is now, banishing Hobson's Conduit to Trumpington Road and clearing out the old market cross.

The river had hitherto received the town's sewage and grew increasingly filthy and evil-smelling. When Queen Victoria asked the Master of Trinity why there were so many pieces of paper in the river he tactfully replied that they were notices forbidding the students to bathe there. The town constructed sewers, sanitation was improved and by the end of the century the river was being used for pleasure. Punting became a Cambridge recreation.

Housing for railway workers built around the turn of the century. Cambridge was a regional railway centre and had large goods yards.

There was an awakening of civic pride. An elaborately decorated corn exchange was built. Houses and shops in the centre of town were rebuilt more solidly and with an extra storey. Stores such as Joshua Taylor and Robert Sayle had their modest beginnings. Bridges were strengthened and Victoria Bridge built for the convenience of new housing north of Midsummer Common. A large new cattle market was provided near the railway station, and the station was linked to the town centre by horse-drawn tramcars. The Guildhall was enlarged to the rear of the eighteenth century building by James Essex, and in 1901 the hated Spinning House was replaced by a splendid new police and fire station, a stone-faced building with much elegant Jacobean strap-work. Concerts were popular, and theatres flourished, though still subject to University surveillance.

The town had grown and was now recognisably modern Cambridge, with an administration that was transformed from the corrupt Mortlock period, all in little more than fifty years. There were widespread slums, some of them near the colleges, but there was also an awakening of a social conscience and a variety of philanthropic societies dedicated to alleviating the problems that the nineteenth century had created.

Punts on the river below Trinity Hall. On a sunny summer's day the river is crowded with punters of all levels of skill.

The Gothic Revival

Though the changes to the town were widespread, it is the University that has left the most memorable, if sometimes intrusive, monuments to the reign of Victoria. University reforms, national prosperity and a steady rise in population all led to a big increase in student numbers. Colleges were now prosperous and some were very wealthy indeed, their estates now producing many times more income, due to wide-spread urban development on their land. All except a handful enlarged their accommodation in the following twenty years. There was no question about the style: the Gothic Revival was at its height and mediaeval colleges deserved no less.

Several of Britain's leading architects were employed. In 1863 St John's turned to Sir George Gilbert Scott for their new chapel, necessary because the old one was in bad repair, and not large enough to hold all the members of the college, who still had to attend compulsorily. Scott's chapel is in the style of the late thirteenth century – the period of the old chapel. It is based on the Abbey Church of Pershore, but with a most un-English polygonal apse, and its shape is that more commonly seen at Oxford, with a western transept and tower above. It is a splendid building, but quite out of scale and character with the rest of the brick court, being much taller, of Ancaster stone and built further north, so that the continuity of the court has disappeared and there is an awkward gap in the street facade. Inside, where the relationship with other buildings is not important, the Victorian decoration is superb; carried out using granite, serpentine and marbles of a variety of colours.

Scott also lengthened the hall, using the space where the Master's Lodge had been, adding a second bay window but using old bricks so that the external appearance does not seem out of place. He then built a new Master's Lodge in the style of a country house with a large garden leading down to the river. Ten years later, Scott added the Chetwynd Building to King's College, and plans were prepared (by him and others) to replace Wilkin's screen with a substantial new building, including a large gate house. No doubt it would have been well-designed and an attractive conception, but visually it would have been a disaster for King's Parade and it is fortunate that it was never built.

Most of Scott's work makes a considerable impact from the street, especially St John's chapel tower, which can be seen from all over Cambridge. So too do some of Alfred Waterhouse's buildings, notably his work for Pembroke and Gonville and Caius. Waterhouse was a flamboyant architect, but he had little concern for existing buildings whatever their merits. Next to Wren's classical chapel at Pembroke, for example, he built a solid residential block in the early French Renaissance style of red brick, with heavy bands of stone, stone window surrounds, tall asymmetrical tower and steeply pitched roof.

Housing for members of the University: left, a don's house to the west of the city, right, St John's Master's Lodge from the river.

Tree Court of Gonville and Caius terminates the famous vista up King's Parade which provided the motive for Waterhouse to design something particularly imposing. It is also in the French Renaissance style with a tower, spire, tall chimneys, statuary and a fine row of water-spouts overlooking Trinity Street. Unlike mediaeval spouts they are not

functional, each being fitted with a neat drainpipe underneath. Both blocks are best from inside their respective courts, where they can be seen without reference to earlier buildings. Like most Victorian additions they had to be on a large scale to provide sufficient accommodation. As he also worked at Jesus, Girton and the Union Society, Waterhouse must have created as great a volume of building as anyone in Cambridge.

Not all Victorian architects were insensitive. George Frederick Bodley has left important works that are much more in keeping with their surroundings. His chapel at Queens' is made of brick like the rest of the college and is of about the same height. It makes an interesting contrast

Portugal Place and the tower of St John's in the background.

Dr Perse's statue in Tree Court, Gonville and Caius. It is believed that he holds a model of the school he founded.

with St John's and, while arguably not as fine, it is much more appropriate as a college chapel. Again the range that Bodley built for King's, overlooking the river, is as large as the Waterhouse blocks but much more in keeping with the rest of King's.

Bodley's finest work in Cambridge was not for a college but for the town. The ancient parish church of All Saints' (once known as All Saints' in the Jewry from the Jewish settlement there up to the thirteenth century) was demolished in 1865. Apart from being in bad condition its western tower projected into Trinity Street where it made difficulties for the increasing traffic. It was rebuilt in Jesus Lane, which by then was a much more convenient centre for the parish, and Bodley designed a beautiful stone-faced chapel in early fourteenth century style, with a tall spire and decorated tracery. Victorian architects often followed a mediaeval pattern but managed to leave their own marks. Bodley placed the tower and spire directly over the chancel, a very unlikely place in a mediaeval church. The site of the earlier church has now been turned into a garden which is used each year by a craft fair.

The Gothic Revival and the related interest in the mediaeval past produced some very mixed results in Cambridge. In 1841 the Round Church was repaired, and under the influence of the Cambridge Camden Society large windows, which had been inserted in the fifteenth century

Bodley's buildings: below, the spire of All Saints' Church, above, the chimneys of the range he built at King's College.

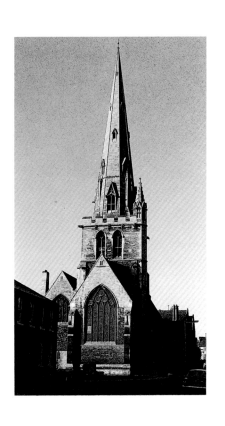

to give more light, were carefully replaced by small ones in the original twelfth century Norman style. A few years later Augustus Wilby Pugin (whose writings had done so much to further the Gothic Revival) removed the great fifteenth century east window of Jesus College chapel and replaced it by five lancet windows to match those surviving on the north and south sides. As a result, the Round Church and Jesus chapel are fine Norman and Early English buildings respectively, but authentic in appearance only.

Some colleges restored Gothic work partly concealed in the eighteenth century when the fashion was for classical architecture. A number of chapels had acquired fine wooden panelling and dignified reredos, with elegantly moulded plaster ceilings. They became more intimate and no doubt warmer. A century later the passion for authentic Gothic removed the reredos, opening up again the large east window and cleared away the plaster to expose the original roof. The wall panelling was however retained. The process can be seen very well at Magdalene: the Ackermann print of 1814 shows the classical appearance of the chapel, while a visit will show the restored original.

Halls, too, followed suit. Emmanuel College hall is now one of the most delightful in the University, the beauty coming to a large degree from the charming grey-blue and white panelling, wrought ironwork in the doorways and lovely plaster ceiling, all put there in the eighteenth century and luckily not removed in the craze for re-establishing Gothic. At Queens' the Old Hall had most of its classical embellishments removed by Bodley in 1861. For the decoration he called in Morris and Co., who painted the roof, stencilled the walls and added attractive tiles over the fireplace. The Old Hall is thus a highly coloured fantasy on a mediaeval hall. In Cambridge there is room for both styles. William Morris, Edward Burne-Jones and their colleagues also worked in Peterhouse, Jesus and in All Saints Church, mainly in stained glass but

The library built by Waterhouse at Pembroke. The oak book stacks and the views of the College gardens contribute to a pleasant working environment.

also in stencil work and tiles. The windows in Jesus College antechapel are a particularly fine and colourful set.

The most extraordinary case of re-Gothicising was at St Catharine's. Because it was felt that a college founded in the Middle Ages ought to have something Gothic, the windows of the classical dining hall were altered into mediaeval ones and an oriel was inserted. The effect is disconcerting.

Education for Women

There were three necessities for a would-be undergraduate before the 1870's: to be a member of the Church of England, to have a considerable income and to be male: three conditions which meant that only a very small section of the population could receive a university education. The first two requirements were eased when the Test Acts were abolished and when the Non-Collegiate Students Board was set up. The education of women at university came at about the same time, after much discussion and pressure.

In 1868 the universities were persuaded to set local examinations for women, so that girls could qualify as teachers. In the following year Emily Davies made the first move towards university education for women by renting Benslow House in Hitchin for herself and five girls. A house in Cambridge was felt to be too close, and so University lecturers had to travel by train to teach the girls in Hitchin. By 1873 numbers had risen so that Benslow House was no longer big enough, and Miss Davies agreed to a move to Cambridge. But still the residence was not to be too close to the centre. For the new college that was to be founded with money raised by her supporters, Emily Davies chose Girton village, two miles away from the town centre, and the college took its name from the village. Emily Davies insisted that women should be taught the same subjects, and in the same way, as men. They were prepared for the same examinations in classics and mathematics, and lecturers still travelled out to Girton, where pupils were chaperoned during tuition.

This was not the only university teaching for women. One of the strongest supporters of women's education in Cambridge was Henry Sidgwick, a well-known philosopher and administrator. He arranged courses of study for five young women whom Anne Jemima Clough gathered together in a house in Regent Street in 1871. Sidgwick and Miss Clough believed that women should have the opportunity of a university education, but that it should be specially designed for them. The group of women lived together as a family, each taking part in the household work. This little group quickly grew and in 1875 a new hall was built at Newnham, and it too took its name from the local village.

Both colleges continued to grow rapidly, and it was not long before two-thirds of the total of thirty-four professors agreed to admit women to their lectures in Cambridge. Sir Arthur Quiller-Couch began all his mixed lectures with "Gentlemen,..." – pointing out that the University still excluded women from full membership.

In 1881 women were allowed to sit the tripos examinations, but they were not awarded degrees. Proposals in the Senate for women to be treated in the same way as men and to be awarded degrees were defeated in 1888 and again eight years later. Both dons and undergraduates were opposed to the idea, even though it was known that some women were performing very well in the examinations. Women's results were

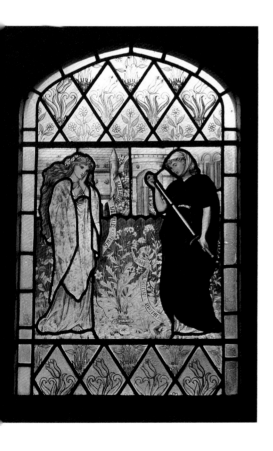

Ariadne and Lucretia, a window in Peterhouse by Burne-Jones, 1869. One of a series illustrating Chaucer's Legends of Good Women.

Girton College, the court built by Waterhouse with the gate tower, its lines now softened by trees.

published in separate pass lists, but it was noted where their names would have appeared in the men's list. In 1890 Philippa Fawcett came first in mathematics and if she had received her due she would have been Senior Wrangler. After lecturing in mathematics for ten years, she left for South Africa to become an educational administrator.

Women had to wait until 1921 before they were allowed to assume the titles of degrees; even then they were not formally awarded. In 1926 women were eligible to take up teaching posts in the faculties. But they were still not full members of the University. Only in 1948 did women achieve that status and with it the right to be awarded degrees in the Senate House. They then found that they were obliged to keep certain regulations that had not previously applied, such as the obligation to wear academic dress on formal occasions.

A third women's college, New Hall, was founded in 1954, in an attempt to rectify the lack of balance between the sexes. But in the last fifteen years the men's colleges have individually voted to admit women students alongside men. Girton College has similarly voted to admit men, and by the autumn of 1987 all colleges admitted both sexes, with the exception of the two women's colleges, Newnham and New Hall. Women now take up about a third of all places. The steady progress of the last fifteen years has been welcomed by colleges but there have been a number for whom the admission of women has been painful. The head porter of one college wore a black tie for a week.

113

Both Girton and Newnham employed eminent architects to design their buildings, Alfred Waterhouse for one and Basil Champneys for the other. Both colleges, too, modified the traditional form of college layout to make the buildings more suitable for young women, including the use of corridors for access to rooms in place of staircases from a court which had its origin in the Middle Ages. In other respects the differences in educational approach between Newnham and Girton are reflected in very different buildings.

Waterhouse, at Girton, built in the imitation Tudor style he had used for other Cambridge colleges with red brick and terracotta. As an indication that Girton was like any other Cambridge college, there are still the traditional components of the mediaeval college: hall, library, chapel and even a gate tower. They are combined in courts and further courts have been made by later additions. The Waterhouse family worked on Girton for several generations: Alfred's son, Paul, succeeded his father by 1890 and in 1931 Paul's son, Michael, was the third generation of Waterhouses to build at Girton. The college has a large site, but the distance from the town which was thought so necessary for preserving conventions in mid-Victorian England is inconvenient for modern university life. Although there is still plenty of space at Girton, the

Men and women students on degree day about to enter the graduation ceremony in the Senate House. A sight that could only have been seen in the last forty of the University's seven hundred years.

Newnham College: its cheerful buildings make a contrast with other Cambridge Victorian college buildings.

college's latest addition, the Wolfson Building, is closer to the town in Clarkson Road.

The first building for Newnham was a large house facing a quiet lane in what was then a remote site some distance away from the town. Old Hall was followed by Sidgwick Hall, nearly opposite, and both were in the domestic Queen Anne style new to Cambridge. They are built of soft red brick with large wooden windows painted white and Dutch gables. Perhaps this domestic style was thought appropriate for women, or if the college did not flourish the buildings could be sold off easily. If so this pessimistic view was proved false, for numbers grew, more houses and a dining hall were built. The lane between the houses was moved and replaced by a beautiful garden and the houses and hall were connected by a walkway. In 1938 the Fawcett Building was designed by the first woman architect to work on a Cambridge college, Elizabeth Whitworth-Scott, and extensions were made to the library in 1981-2 by another woman architect, Joanna van Keyningan. Seen from the garden the lovely brick and woodwork make Newnham College one of the most charming of all Cambridge colleges. The erection of Selwyn College and twentieth century building for University lecture rooms and libraries nearby makes Newnham much closer to a significant part of the University.

Eminent Edwardians

After the changes brought about by the Royal Commission and the reforms which followed it, the student population increased five-fold in the eighty years from 1802, rising from not much over six hundred to over three thousand. Colleges were now offering much wider fields of study, with a more serious approach to scholarship and firmer discipline imposed by the University. Men used their time at the universities to qualify for professional employment.

Cambridge was helping dispel the reputation England had acquired of being the "land without music". Two gifted composers, who were also fine teachers, William Sterndale-Bennett and Charles Villiers Stanford, were paving the way for a new wave of English composers, of whom Ralph Vaughan Williams of Trinity was perhaps the best known.

There were no literary figures to match those earlier in the century. Charles Kingsley became Professor of History in 1860, and his novels were very popular in his own day. *Alton Lock* has many references to Cambridge. *Hereward the Wake* is one of the few books to romanticise the damp and gloomy Fens to the north of the town. Other writers in Cambridge at this time include Samuel Butler (author of *The Way of All Flesh* and *Erewhon*) and two novelists who achieved recognition in the twentieth century, E. M. Forster and John Cowper Powys.

E. M. Forster, of King's, has been one of the most influential English writers of the twentieth century and winner of the Nobel Prize for Literature. His output was small, but carefully written. In later years he came back to Cambridge and lived in college until his death, doing little work but willing to spend much of his time talking to students. Powys has not received the attention he deserves: his novels are long and rambling, but with a sense of mystery and epic grandeur. With fewer ambitions, A. A. Milne of Trinity has enriched the lives of an infinitely greater number of people with his *Winnie the Pooh* stories. One of his manuscripts is now exhibited in the Wren Library.

A group of friends who became known as the Bloomsbury Set attracted most attention at this time. They included Lytton Strachey, Clive Bell and Leonard Woolf. Lytton Strachey's best-known work *Eminent Victorians* established a scorn for Victorian life and values which persisted until the 1950's. The greatest writer in the group, Virginia Stephen, married Leonard Woolf but was not at the University. Another member of this group was Maynard Keynes, who came up to King's College in 1902 where he later developed his theories of economics. Keynes had wide interests; he collected post-impressionist pictures, paid for the building of the Arts Theatre which opened in Cambridge in 1936, made successful changes to the finances of King's and, after the Second World War, took a prominent role in organising Marshall Aid for Europe.

Petty Cury on a Saturday morning. Lloyds Bank, another building by the Waterhouse firm, in the background.

Ede and Ravenscroft, probably the oldest firm of tailors in the world. It has held royal appointments to thirteen British monarchs from William and Mary to the present day.

In the early twentieth century Cambridge was an intellectually exciting place. The Union Society provided a platform for young men to make reputations as speakers, and was a step towards a political career University periodicals, such as *The Cambridge Review* and *The Granta*, offered aspiring writers an opportunity to display their talents. College plays and entertainments abounded. It had become the fashion to be noticed and stand out from the growing numbers.

The Apostles probably contained more illustrious members during this period than either before or since. Its members included G. L. Dickinson, J. M. Keynes, Roger Fry, G. M. Trevelyan, the genial King's don Oscar Browning, Lytton Strachey, Leonard Woolf, and the philosophers Bertrand Russell, A. N. Whitehead and G. E. Moore.

It was an age of much wit, some elegance and, in retrospect, a touch of sadness, for these were the last days of leisure and innocence. The grim days of the First World War were at hand. Perhaps the person who crystallised best the spirit of the time was Rupert Brooke. As an undergraduate at King's, Brooke did all the things a bright young man should. He wrote and discussed poetry, acted in college plays, made suitable friends and enjoyed life to the full. Like thousands of other young men he did not hesitate to join the army in 1914, confident that he was embarking upon a great and exciting adventure. He was to die overseas, not in battle but of illness, on a remote Greek island. His famous sonnet summed up popular feeling in the early days of the war, but it is his longer poem on Grantchester that conveys best his nostalgia for good times now gone. Grantchester and Rupert Brooke together symbolise a golden age now vanished.

Chapter 8

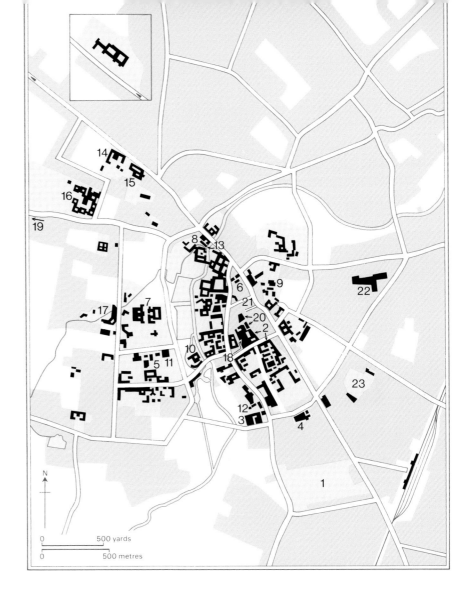

Town sites
University sites

*The view towards Cambridge
from Grantchester Meadows. The
footpath to Grantchester has
nostalgic memories for
generations of Cambridge people.*

The Growth of Departments and Colleges

The twentieth century has seen great changes in the University. There are now more than twelve thousand students, including postgraduates; before the Second World War there were fewer than half the present number of students. This has largely been brought about by the Education Act of 1944 which gave financial assistance to almost all British university students, enabling even the poorest to benefit from a university education. Despite the establishment of many more universities, there is intense competition for places at Cambridge, and admission is based more on academic ability than ever before. For the first time there is a majority of students from the maintained schools.

The more democratic selection of students has been accompanied by a gradual increase in freedom for both senior members and undergraduates. There is more informality in dress and behaviour. The colleges have become more comfortable. Electricity was introduced in

The Apostles in 1932. From the left, Richard Llewellyn-Davies, Hugh Sykes Davies, Alistair Watson, Anthony Blunt, Julian Bell, Andrew Cohen.

Opposite: aspects of Cambridge, above, after a May Ball, below jokes abound.

the 1890's, first at Peterhouse by Lord Kelvin, and gradually student accommodation has been modernised. More dons live out of college in family homes, but retain rooms in college for tutorial purposes.

There are hundreds of clubs and societies covering an extraordinarily wide range of interests as diverse as those for "the survival of tribal peoples" and the "preservation of the strawberry in Cambridge". The standard of music is now very high and college choirs are among the best in the world. Competitive sport between colleges reaches a climax in the "bumps" races during May Week. To celebrate the week May Balls were held, starting in the 1890's. They are now held in June, after examinations, although still known as May Balls.

As the number of subjects grew, so did faculty buildings to house them. The Botanical Gardens were moved in 1852 from their central site to their present position between Trumpington Street and Hills Road. The adjacent site of the Perse Grammar School was also obtained. The sites were used for a muddle of departmental buildings and their heavy mixed classical and Tudor facades dominate Downing Street. The northern part of the Downing site, sold to the University in 1906, was developed around a central street for departmental offices, museums and

laboratories. Despite the interesting and high quality detail of some of the individual buildings, the effect of these two sites is confusing, and contrasts sharply with the clarity of the colleges. No doubt this is due to their rapid growth and the competing demands of departments.

Growing departments were again rehoused on sites progressively further from the centre. The University Engineering Department was built near Coe Fen in stages between 1930 and 1960. A large dull block was built also in southern Cambridge to house the Chemical Laboratories in 1950. The Arts Faculties, built to the west of the river, had an overall plan prepared by Casson & Condor who also designed many of the picturesque buildings on the site. On the same site and in complete contrast, James Stirling designed the History Faculty, for a long time the most controversial building in Cambridge. Its uncompromising form is based around the radial book stacks, arranged in a quadrant, under a "tent" of glass slung between the office blocks on either side.

The University Library, one of three "copyright libraries" in Britain, was growing fast and in 1931 The Rockefeller Foundation gave funds for a new building. Giles Gilbert Scott's monolithic tower has now been accepted as part of the western Cambridge skyline. The University Press, still in the Pitt Building, was relocated in 1980 to larger premises in south Cambridge. In 1985 it had more books on its list than any other publisher – 840 titles.

The History Faculty library, 1964, designed by James Stirling. An influential design in stark contrast to the picturesque buildings in the Sidgwick Arts Faculty.

The wide area over which University departments are now spread makes a bicycle essential for undergraduates and dons. They are found stacked in every conceivable position in Cambridge. The first bicycle seems to have been seen in the 1860's ridden by a Trinity man and many still in use appear to date from not long after. The bicycle's traditional freedom in the Cambridge streets is now being endangered by the car.

All colleges have provided more residences for their undergraduates,because of the substantial rise in numbers and social changes which have made it difficult for students to find lodgings in the town. During the 1950's the colleges restarted the tradition of using contemporary architects and Cambridge is one of the best places in the country to see their work. This is not accidental, for the colleges were able to afford good quality building and architects have always accepted the challenge of building alongside revered creations of the past.

The first building in the "international modern" style was the Erasmus Building at Queens' by Basil Spence which generated many angry letters to *The Times* in the late 1950's with its cuboid shape and irregular windows. Now it appears a moderate design, its brick conforms with the older parts of the college, and it is hard to see what caused offence.

The sites of many of the older colleges were quickly exhausted and much ingenuity has been shown to use every inch of space, for instance at Corpus Christi where an extra storey was added to Wilkins' Court. A more recent and less damaging example is at Trinity, where Architect's Co-Partnership erected a five storey residence block on top of Heffer's bookshop and Sainsbury's supermarket. This new Wolfson Building, being surrounded by offices, does not intrude upon the town. Even local people often have no idea of its existence.

Clare took the first step in extending westwards across the Cam in 1924 and built Memorial Court, an quiet brick court in a neo-classical style by Giles Gilbert Scott, into which a new college library has recently been inserted. The Cripps Building of St John's starts at the Cam at the back of New Court, crosses Bin Brook and ends near the Pythagoras Building. Accommodation is provided for two hundred – more than four times the number in the sixteenth century college. It is faced with Portland stone and built in sections that form small courts to break up its considerable length. Powell and Moya have produced a serviceable building which is also pleasing to look at. Denys Lasdun's New Court at Christ's creates a completely different effect. Here seven terraces of rooms, all facing south, descend in steps, a grand spectacle when seen approaching through the College, but ugly on the town side where its car-park entrance is in King Street.

The Cripps Building, St John's College, designed by Powell and Moya, 1966. The building winds its way from the Cam behind New Court, across Bin Brook, to the School of Pythagoras.

Much ingenuity has been shown to make new buildings fit traditional court layouts. Harvey Court for Gonville and Caius was designed by Leslie Martin (Professor of Architecture at the University) to demonstrate the benefits of low-rise building and has been influential. In contrast the same architect's William Stone building in Peterhouse is a beautifully detailed tower block isolated far away across the Deer Park. Most ingenious of all, King's and St Catharine's employed Fello Atkinson to prepare a joint plan for new accommodation over and on both sides of King's Lane without spoiling roof-lines. The Lane itself is even more unsightly than before.

Magdalene started to build a new court across Magdalene Street in 1930, and one long range was built by Sir Edwin Lutyens, his only work in the town. Lutyens created a solid structure with elegant details. A second range would perhaps have been too forbidding and in the early 1950's a new approach was adopted by adapting existing mediaeval buildings and adding a few small new buildings to make this part of Magdalene one of the most interesting in the University. The architects, David Roberts and Geoffrey Clarke, have also carried out much other work in the town including the extension to the Fitzwilliam Museum.

Harvey Court, Gonville and Caius on the west bank sited in gardens once belonging to the houses built for dons in the nineteenth century.

A revival of an old approach to college building. Lutyens' second block in Magdalene's Mallory Court would have swept away these sixteenth century houses. David Roberts converted them into student accommodation.

In the four new colleges the architects have been able to rethink the buildings required to serve college life. The traditional prominence of the chapel has been challenged. As often in their history, the colleges have been obliged by the funds available to build in stages, but their architects have attempted to design for future growth. Fitzwilliam College required the traditional "majestic scale" and Denys Lasdun designed one large central area containing communal facilities such as hall and library. Residential buildings are planned to grow in a spiral around it as funds are found. At New Hall Peter Chamberlin planned a covered walkway as an axis. College buildings join to it on either side. The hall is in the form of a Greek cross covered by a flamboyant dome. The library faces it across a court containing a pool. All is white – brick and concrete.

Churchill, the largest of the new colleges, was founded to foster science and by statute over two-thirds of its members are scientists. Richard Sheppard placed the communal rooms in two central groups and the accommodation in ten courts arranged in groups, which for the first time included flats for married Fellows. The strong building forms in brick and concrete provide an impression of strength and durability. At the insistence of the Fellows, who included Francis Crick, the chapel was placed at the far side of the playing fields. Most recently Robinson College, completed in 1980, is planned in two rings, the outer containing

New Hall, Cambridge's third college for women, designed by Chamberlin, Powell and Bon, built in 1962. The excitement of the 1960's geared to the identity of a new college.

offices, chapel and library, the inner containing students' rooms and hall. Robinson was the first college to be planned for both men and women and also for use as a conference centre during vacations. The architects, Andy Macmillan and Izi Metzstein, constructed it of brickwork and the garden at the back benefits from mature trees, once in the gardens of dons' houses. The college has a pleasant social atmosphere and is liked by its residents.

To meet a growing need the University has also provided better for mature students and postgraduates. Postgraduates had always been accommodated in colleges and mature students are now often accepted. A number of colleges especially for postgraduates and mature students, Clare Hall, Wolfson, Lucy Cavendish and Darwin Colleges, were founded in the 1960's all in west Cambridge. Darwin College has extended the previous home of the Darwin family on the river near the mill. Ralph Erskine designed an interesting building for Clare Hall containing flats, houses and common rooms separated by courts. These and other extensive developments on the west bank of the Cam have now changed the nature of the Backs. It has effectively become a central campus for the University.

The University's royal connections continue; there have been royal benefactors from Edward II for seven centuries. The present Prince of Wales went to Trinity and his brother Prince Edward to Jesus College.

A residential court in Churchill College, 1961, designed by Richard Sheppard. A large college with two-thirds of the members scientists. Trees have lightened the powerful forms.

Growth of Science

The growth of science at Cambridge during the past hundred years has been perhaps the greatest development in the history of the University. Even in the days of William Whewell, Master of Trinity in the mid-nineteenth century, no regular course of instruction existed and any practical work undertaken was carried out in private laboratories. The Natural History Tripos established in 1848 provided the starting point but it was some time before anything substantial was achieved. Impetus came from the founding of the Cavendish Laboratory in 1873, the gift of the Duke of Devonshire who succeeded Prince Albert as Chancellor. Henry Cavendish was a distinguished eighteenth century scientist from a branch of the Duke's family. When the Cavendish opened, there were nineteen students in the natural sciences. The first two professors, J. Clerk Maxwell and Lord Rayleigh, organised lectures and practical work, and encouraged individual research. Maxwell worked on electricity and magnetism and explained the theory of radio waves before their practical discovery. Lord Rayleigh discovered argon and other inert gases.

Above, James Clerk Maxwell, one of the first two professors at the Cavendish. Below, J. J. Thompson, discoverer of the electron.

In 1884 J. J. Thompson became Cavendish Professor, and for over thirty years he directed the Laboratory. More than any other man he was responsible for the fundamental change in physics during this century. Numbers working in the Laboratory rose, and the approach to theoretical and experimental work was consolidated although apparatus was limited and frequently had to be improvised. Thompson

*Above, Rutherford in the
Cavendish Laboratory.
Below, the crocodile carved by
Eric Gill on the Mond Building.*

discovered the electron and worked on the conductivity of electricity through gases. Shortly after Thompson's appointment, the University allowed graduates of other universities to receive a degree in two years if they submitted a thesis on an approved subject. As a result men came from other British universities and abroad to carry out research in Cambridge. One was Ernest Rutherford from New Zealand who was financed by funds from the Great Exhibition of 1851.

Thompson resigned in 1919 to become Master of Trinity College and he was succeeded by Rutherford. For eighteen years Rutherford dominated physics in Cambridge. Equipment was now more readily available and cyclotrons and high-voltage accelerators were installed. Rutherford was the first to explain the structure of the atom and to carry out experiments to prove his theories, work which has now come to be known as "splitting the atom". Further discoveries were made by the talented scientists and research students whom he had assembled in the Cavendish. John Cockcroft, James Chadwick and a Russian, Peter Kapitza, were among them; Rutherford was interested in everybody's work and always available with advice. The Mond Laboratory was built in the courtyard facing the Cavendish for Kapitza, who was doing research into the characteristics of materials in intense magnetic fields. On the new Mond building Eric Gill carved the image of a crocodile, Kapitza's nickname for Rutherford, perhaps because Rutherford's voice could be heard before he came into sight as the crocodile's alarm clock could in *Peter Pan*.

It is hard to grasp that the progression from elementary lectures to atomic science took only half a century. Teaching and research were revolutionised in this time. Prior to the Second World War Cambridge research had been reinforced by the arrival of talented scientists seeking refuge from Germany and Austria. After the Second World War Cambridge's lead in atomic physics declined. Much Cambridge expertise had been exported to the United States and used in the British development of radar as part of the war effort. Sir Lawrence Bragg had worked on X-ray diffraction and decided to concentrate the energies of the Cavendish on the use of these methods in molecular biology. Again the results were impressive and the list of names includes J. D. Watson and F. C. H. Crick who made the final breakthrough in the description of the structure of DNA as a double helix in 1953. The Laboratory's work led to great advances in medicine, and a separate Molecular Biology Laboratory was set up in the 1960's. Later work in the Cavendish includes Nevill Mott's description of the functioning of semi-conducting materials has great significance for the development of new electronic components.

A second application of physics has been in radio astronomy, the study of stars and galaxies by recording the faint radio waves they emit. Large dishes to collect and focus the radio waves are needed. By ingenious design Martin Ryle constructed the equivalent of a radio telescope with a five kilometer dish using a series of movable smaller dishes on a disused railway track, to the south of Cambridge. With the telescopes a colleague, Anthony Hewish, discovered pulsars and quasars. After the pioneering work of Babbage on mechanical computers in the first half of the eighteenth century, Maurice Wilkes of the University's Mathematical Laboratory designed an early electronic computer and set up the Computing Laboratory. Further work of great influence on the design of computers and their applications has been produced in the Laboratory.

In 1973, one hundred years after its first founding, the Cavendish Laboratory moved to new buildings to the west of Cambridge, designed to accommodate large experimental equipment by moving interior walls and floors. The Laboratory continues to be in the forefront of scientific research. Over twenty-five Nobel prizes have been won in this single laboratory, and about the same number in other departments, making a total of over fifty for the University. Most have been in the sciences which, in Cambridge University, have been taught and researched systematically for only just over a hundred years. No doubt further discoveries of importance to mankind will be made in the future.

Below, the linear radio telescopes of Martin Ryle.

A well-known spot for a traffic tangle; in term-time the cars take second place.

Mowbrays' bookshop seen from St Edward's churchyard.

A Crowded Tapestry

The town has also changed and its population figures provide a clue: just over nine thousand in 1801, fifty-five thousand in 1905 and approaching one hundred and ten thousand today. The bulk of the town belongs to the last hundred years: housing for the added tens of thousands with the schools, churches and shops also needed.

To cater for regional needs there have been two major central shopping developments. The first was the Lion Yard development in the early 1970's when old property including one side of Petty Cury was rebuilt as shops, with a multi-storey car park and a public library. Many people regretted the virtual destruction of Petty Cury and its atmosphere of old Cambridge but the shopping facilities are now heavily used. Ten years later, after fierce controversy, an area of run-down housing and small shops known as the Kite was developed as the Grafton Centre, a large shopping precinct with its own car park, which would in theory take pressure off the historic centre.

Civic awareness has grown since the the town has run its own affairs and became a City in 1951. The Guildhall was rebuilt in the 1930's in stone and brick. It is grand in scale but pleasantly proportioned. In the 1870's a Corn Exchange was built to serve the needs of farmers in Cambridgeshire. Recently its coloured brickwork has been cleaned, the interior refitted and on re-opening in 1986 is proving a versatile entertainment centre. The most pressing and seemingly intractable problem in the city centre is traffic control. The real difficulty lies in the mediaeval pattern of narrow streets. Recent traffic planning has reduced car access to the central area and proposed car-parks on the periphery of the city with public transport into the centre.

Rose Crescent, student rooms above the shops and restaurants.

The old friction between Town and Gown continues though in a more subdued way. The privilege of students is still resented and there are areas which are used by one more than the other. Since the 1940's the distinction between term and vacation has completely changed. Once when term ended and the students went home, Cambridge became very quiet. For some time the colleges have seen that conferences, some of which relate to University studies, provide income and keep their staff occupied, while at the same time giving many people the pleasure of staying in college rooms. In addition some twenty English language schools now operate within the city. Their students flock into the city centre together with the tourists in the summer. In 1986 nearly four million tourists were estimated to have been in Cambridge, and most will have visited King's College Chapel and Trinity College. Such large numbers cause problems for the central colleges, and they are increasing.

The four million tourists bring problems but they bring prosperity too. People come because they want to see a city with more beautiful buildings than any in Britain of comparable size. Many come from the United States to see where Harvard studied before he sailed for New England, or the Cavendish Laboratory where the atom 'was split and DNA deciphered. There is a thrill in seeing the pulpits where Fisher, Ridley and Latimer preached or the court at Christ's where Milton and Darwin had rooms on opposite sides, though separated by two centuries. It is easy to imagine how the young Victoria must have seen it on her first visit with the formal elegance of King's caught in the morning light across the meadows. Everywhere there are reminders of people who have enriched Cambridge and the world through the centuries and these reminders in turn enrich those who come to live or visit.

An August Sunday on King's Parade.

Chapter 9
by Nick Segal

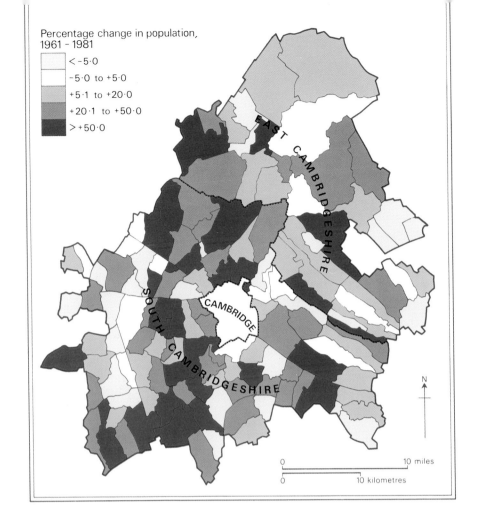

Percentage change in population, 1961 - 1981

- < -5·0
- -5·0 to +5·0
- +5·1 to +20·0
- +20·1 to +50·0
- > +50·0

EAST CAMBRIDGESHIRE

SOUTH CAMBRIDGESHIRE

CAMBRIDGE

N

| 0 | | 10 miles |
| 0 | | 10 kilometres |

Population has not increased in Cambridge but extremely rapidly in the area within ten to twenty miles of the City.

The view across one of the three lakes in the Trinity College Science Park. Trinity has owned the land used for the Park since 1443.

Introduction

Cambridge has occupied a privileged position in British and, especially, English life for centuries. Earlier chapters have shown the many dimensions of this at different periods and in different ways: the connections with the Church, the arts, the land, industry, government, science and medicine. There can be few aspects of the nation's history and of its internationally recognised achievements in which Cambridge dons and graduates have not played a prominent part. The physical beauty of the city's mediaeval centre – the river meandering through the colleges, the college buildings themselves, the Backs – has exerted a special and enduring hold on many generations of undergraduates and their families and also on large numbers of tourists, British and now increasingly foreign.

Small wonder then that the name Cambridge has a cachet, national and international. In Britain only Oxford can rival such a prestigious reputation – but it is not for an Oxford graduate, writing about Cambridge, to judge the relative claims of each.

Earlier chapters have shown too that since mediaeval times Cambridge has essentially been a university and a market town, set in a somewhat bleak and remote rural environment. The turbulent pressures of the industrial revolution largely by-passed Cambridge – arrival of the railways in the town was one of the few but not drastic exceptions. There was extensive poverty in the countryside and in the town too, because of the low wages and the lack of job opportunities outside agriculture and college or domestic service. Nevertheless the prevailing picture over many years has been one of privilege, power and affluence, and of exceptional talent and ability among numerous individuals.

This is the traditional image of Cambridge, and it still endures. But against this backcloth something new has entered the Cambridge scene: high technology industry. Public awareness, even locally, of this new arrival has emerged only in the 1980's. But, as will be seen shortly, the first high technology companies themselves go back many decades and, more significantly, the ultimate origins of the new industry lie directly in the general conditions and characteristics that have made Cambridge such a distinctive place.

The growth of high technology industry has itself had distinctive features. It has been a "homespun" development dependent in the first instance on the enterprise and energy of local organisations and individuals, notably including those in the academic community. It has been spearheaded too by locally formed small firms. These are characteristics that are prized by politicians and planners not only elsewhere in Britain but throughout the industrialised world.

For all these reasons the Cambridge Phenomenon – as this growth of high technology industry has come to be known – is now widely celebrated. The Phenomenon has derived prestige from its association with Cambridge, but equally it has reinforced and extended the reputation of Cambridge itself.

This chapter is about the Phenomenon: what it comprises, how it has come about and why in Cambridge, what changes it is bringing to the city, and what the future might hold. The story, especially with all its ramifications, is a large and complex one: and the present essay is a modest distillation of what has been written elsewhere.

Early Beginnings

In 1878 a scientific instruments firm was set up in Cambridge to exploit the local market for scientific instruments created by the rapid growth of the University's recently established departments of experimental physics – the Cavendish Laboratory – and of physiology. The firm was formed in semi-association with the newly appointed first incumbent of the chair of "mechanism", and its first workshop was to grow into the University's engineering laboratories.

The two founders of the firm – one Albert Dew-Smith, a recent local graduate; the other Robert Fulcher, a mechanic trained in London – had insufficient knowledge of engineering and of the major advances being made in many scientific and industrial fields, principally in Germany, the USA and Britain, to build a business that could go beyond meeting the needs of the local scientific market. Consequently, while the firm flourished for a few years, it needed an infusion of new ideas and greater breadth. These qualities were provided in the form of Horace Darwin (the youngest surviving son of Charles), an 1874 graduate of the University with a flair for instrument design and with ready access to the latest results and the instrument needs of the University's laboratories. In 1881 a new partnership was established between Darwin and Dew-Smith, which brought into being the Cambridge Scientific Instrument Company – undoubtedly the first company in the Phenomenon, and surely one of the earliest and longest-surviving university-linked companies in the world.

Under Darwin's leadership and, eventually, sole ownership, the Instrument Company diversified successfully into industrial as well as other scientific markets world-wide, and was one of the founders of the British instruments industry. A remarkable early record was established including design and production of the world's first seismograph and commercial automatic temperature controller; later achievements included development of transmission and scanning electron microscope technology undertaken, as in many other instances, in collaboration with the University. Cambridge Instruments (as the company is now called) has experienced varying fortunes over the years, as well as a complex history of corporate change including a series of government sponsored mergers in the 1960's and 1970's with a number of instrument and other companies. One of the latter may also be counted as an early Phenomenon firm: Metals Research, an exceptionally exciting science-based enterprise that had "spun out" from the University's Metallurgy Department in 1957.

The 1980's have seen renewed vitality in Cambridge Instruments, brought about by introduction of international capital and management, and an accompanying transformation from a craft-based tradition to highly sophisticated methods of design and production of scientific, medical and industrial instruments.

In 1896 a second company was established in Cambridge to supply laboratory equipment for educational, scientific and industrial purposes. The founder was W. G. Pye, the chief mechanic at the Cavendish who had earlier served his apprenticeship at the Scientific Instrument Company. This company, too, and its many offshoots have a record of distinguished achievements – pioneering the development of radio and television technology, radar and other detection systems and also medical instruments in the inter-war period, and of hi-fi systems and telecommunications and analytical instruments after the Second World War. But Pye's fortunes too have fluctuated over the years and after World War Two it was acquired by the Dutch corporation Philips. Today, after many complex changes, the substantial legacy of Pye is a free-standing conglomerate: Cambridge Electronic Industries and a set

Graeme Minto, Cambridge engineering graduate and founder, now chairman, of Domino Printing Sciences, a 1978 spin-out from CCL.

of Philips subsidiaries. Together they continue to exercise a sizeable influence on the Cambridge scene.

Another of the early University-linked and science-based companies was called Aero Research, a synthetic resins manufacturer set up in 1934. Its founder was Norman de Bruyne, Senior Bursar of Trinity College and a researcher at the Cavendish; and its product was a high performance glue which de Bruyne had invented while collaborating with Marshalls (the local aircraft engineering and vehicles company, whose principals were recent engineering graduates of the University) in development of the Mosquito aircraft. Aero Research was taken over by the Swiss concern Ciba Geigy in 1948; de Bruyne later started up a new scientific instruments firm, Techne, based in Cambridge and Princeton; and in 1968, Ciba Geigy also set up an agro-chemicals facility in the area.

In 1960 a new enterprise, Cambridge Consultants Limited (CCL), was established with the aim of supplying high quality technical and design services to manufacturing industry. The firm was the brainchild of Tim Eiluart, a recent chemical engineering graduate of the University, and its rationale and marketing pitch were to capitalise explicitly on the firm's Cambridge origins and connections and on its ability to recruit exceptionally talented graduates. Numerous outstanding individuals who have contributed significantly to the country's business and technological development have been "products" of CCL; and it was through a personal link with with Eiluart that Clive Sinclair developed business connections with Cambridge and made it his base from 1967. CCL's early history was somewhat chequered, and in the 1960's it went through several crises. But it grew and achieved a substantial reputation and after severe financial difficulties had ensued it was bought by Arthur D. Little, the Boston Research and Development (R&D) and consultancy firm. Although retaining a high degree of autonomy, CCL has gone from strength to strength since the take-over.

CCL has, directly and indirectly, been a prolific source of spin-out companies (now numbering well over thirty) in the Cambridge area. In the 1960's this was generally due to frustration on the part of the spin-out entrepreneurs; but from the late 1970's CCL positively encouraged staff to do their own thing if they so wished. One of the most successful of these spin-outs has been Domino Printing Sciences, set up in 1978 and now a world leader in ink-jet printing technology. Another interesting spin-out has been Prelude Technology Investments, set up in 1985 by CCL itself and with an initial fund of £5 million raised from City of London institutions, to finance and assist young technology enterprises being established in Cambridge or elsewhere.

The history of these early companies – Cambridge Instruments, Pye and its various components, Aero Research, the Coles brother's firm Metals Research, and Cambridge Consultants – gives a clear pointer to some of the things that were to start happening on a larger scale and at an accelerating pace from the late 1960's onwards:

* local formation of firms by talented and enterprising individuals with specialist know-how derived from their research in the University and from experience gained in other firms;

* appearance of niche market opportunities (arising from the presence of the University or other large organisations as buyers) open to new firms because of the absence of established suppliers;

* acquisition by larger, invariably foreign, companies of the small local enterprises once they had performed successfully and grown beyond a certain size.

First Growth

It is the post-1960's business developments – leading to the presence of some 450-500 high technology companies in the area in 1987 – that have become popularly known in the 1980's as the Cambridge Phenomenon. But it is important also to recognise the early origins of the Phenomenon as well as its dependence on such chance contextual factors as the small size and remoteness of Cambridge, the limited earlier industrialisation, the lack of employment opportunities for graduates who wanted to stay in the area and so on.

Such factors as these – reinforced by the sustained pre-eminence throughout this century of the University and associated research institutions in many disciplines – created for many years an exceptionally fertile environment for development of science-based businesses. Many elements have made up this "pre-conditioning". Some have been highly specific to Cambridge: for example, the Government's 1968 decision to establish the national Computer-Aided Design Centre here, which unintentionally has been an important source of new firm formation.

Other factors have been more general. Examples include the national revival of the small firms sector starting, albeit slowly and uncertainly, in the early 1970's; the fact of East Anglia becoming the country's fastest growing region from about 1960, and sustaining that performance right up to the present; and, above all, from the 1970's the massive improvements in the strategic road communications serving the Cambridge area, notably the M11 motorway on the north-south axis (bringing London nearer in time, convenience and perception) and the A45 on the east-west axis (connecting Cambridge to the east coast ports and to the industrial West Midlands).

The list of factors causing and shaping in a strategic sense the growth of high technology industry in Cambridge could be greatly extended and its variety readily demonstrated. There is no need to recite them all, but one set of events must be briefly recounted.

Up to about the mid-nineteenth century Cambridge was no more than a university and market town and, more recently in the period, a regional

Dr Bob Hook, a Cambridge physicist, formerly a director of CCL and now managing director of the venture capital firm Prelude Technology Investments, itself a 1985 CCL spin-out.

rail centre. In the second half of the century growth started taking place, due partly to expansion of the University itself and partly to the impact of the railways. The city's population at the turn of the century was nearly 50,000, having been about 20,000 in 1830.

Growth continued in the first half of the present century: by 1951 the population had reached nearly 90,000 (and that of the so-called "inner ring" villages nearly 19,000). This growth was the outcome of several factors: the success of Cambridge Instruments, Pye and Marshalls (in some measure because of the Second World War); the city's taking on a new role in the war as a regional base for some departments of central government; further expansion of the University in many directions, with several departments such as physics and biochemistry being among the world's leaders; and the establishment locally of several national research institutions linked in some way to the University (examples include the Plant Breeding Institute, National Institute of Agricultural Botany, Institute of Animal Physiology, Institute of Animal Nutrition, and the Welding Institute).

This growth, and especially the industrialisation, were not universally welcomed in Cambridge. There were fears that the city's traditional character would be irretrievably changed. Should not growth, if it had to happen, be channeled to the rural hinterland which was then in decline? This view applied all the more strongly to growth of manufacturing – development of the car industry at Cowley on the outskirts of Oxford was seen as indicative of the disharmonious impact, socially and physically, of industry on a university town.

These fears in Cambridge were shared at national level. A special team was set up under William Holford to prepare a city plan for Cambridge. The fundamental premises of this exercise were that Cambridge should remain predominantly a university town, that any significant expansion was incompatible with this and would damage the very qualities that made Cambridge a special place, and that growth should be encouraged in outer villages and more distant market towns.

The Holford plan was published in 1950 and endorsed by central government in 1954. Its impact was strong and protracted; its benefits and also its legacy of restrictive thinking survive today. The immediate outcome was the imposition of tight planning policies, subsequently reinforced by the drawing of a "green belt" closely around the northern limits of Cambridge and the inner villages as well as by a variety of other negative measures.

These restrictions had a discernible effect on the location of industry. For instance, in the 1950's Tube Investments wished to establish its new R&D laboratories in Cambridge because of its connections with the Engineering and Physics Departments; this was disallowed and the laboratories were instead set up ten miles away. In the 1960's Metals Research and PA Technology (a 1970 CCL spin-out) were denied

Dr Ian Nicol, Cambridge physicist who, before becoming Secretary-General of the University's Board of Faculties, was the driving force behind the establishment of the Mott Committee.

Professor Roger Needham, currently head of the University's Computer Laboratory and one of the founding directors of CCL in 1960.

permission to expand in Cambridge itself, and both relocated to Melbourn where since the late 1970's Metals Research's premises have formed the nucleus of a successful science park development. Also in the 1960's, and the best known and most controversial of all, was the planning authorities' refusal to allow IBM to establish its European R&D laboratories in Cambridge.

Such negative planning attitudes – understandable at the time, especially when industry was widely regarded as "smokestack" – can with hindsight be seen as going against the grain of change already under way in Cambridge. Not only were there science-based business developments of the kind already described; the University itself had continued to expand and its research reputation was growing in major new fields such as molecular biology and computer applications, and new laboratories were being established in medical and related fields.

More significantly, a few key individuals in the University saw at the time the potential damage to the University's own long-term interests of restrictive planning policies. Influenced by what was happening around Stanford and MIT in the USA, and aware of the long-term trends in funding and organisation of British science, they believed that the vitality and relevance of their own work and of Cambridge's teaching and research more generally would be enhanced if there were in the geographic vicinity a number and diversity of science-based industrial companies and non-academic research institutions. They were encouraged too by central government's exhortations about society realising the benefits of "the white-hot technological revolution". These individuals lobbied the University to act.

In 1967 the University set up a committee to "consider in greater detail and advise on the planning aspects of the relationship between the University and science-based industry". It took two years before the report of this committee (whose chairman was Nevill Mott, head of the Cavendish) was approved by the Senate. But its conclusions and recommendations were unambiguous: "The root of the problems" underlying its own commissioning lay in the uncritical application of the "Holford principles... formulated on the basis of population forecasts well below those generally accepted and a rate of University expansion smaller than had in fact taken place." The report observed that planning restrictions based on Holford's plan had created recruitment difficulties for the University in addition to imposing even more severe restrictions on industrial and other growth not immediately connected with the University.

In looking ahead, the Mott report concluded that it would be in the interests of the local economy and the University to encourage a limited growth of existing and new science-based industry and applied research units in and near Cambridge. Initially it recommended that a science park be created in Cambridge, capable of housing up to 2,000 employees, which would offer the right physical and planning environment for science-based industry and would be accessible to University departments and the wider research community. The Mott report was, after much argument, understood and accepted locally. It marks a watershed in the evolution of the University's official attitudes to academic links with industry and, along with the planning authorities, also to local industrial development. It helped to clarify the distinction between smokestack and science-based industry and it legitimised the role of the latter as an integral element in the future of the University's research and the Cambridge scene generally.

The first outward sign of the University authorities' changed attitudes to industry was when they allowed Laser-Scan, a computer graphics company formed in 1969 by three researchers at the Cavendish, temporary accommodation in spare laboratory space. But by far the most important sign, and indeed the most vital consequence of that report, was the decision by Trinity College in 1970 to establish a science park on a 130 acre block of land on the north-eastern edge of the city some three miles from the centre. The Cambridge Science Park took its first tenant, Laser-Scan, in 1973 and, after a slow first several years, lettings have proceeded quickly in the 1980's. In mid-1987 there were some 65 tenants occupying nearly 60,000 square metres (an increase of some 60% over the previous three years), and the scheme, now in its final phase of development, is established as the leading university science park in Britain if not Europe.

That it was Trinity College that responded positively to the Mott report has been fortunate. Not only did it have a suitable block of land (with few other options for its use) in what has become an excellent location well serviced by the new motorway and trunk road system; but Trinity more than any other college also had the financial resources and the experience to drive the scheme through, as well as the patience to take a long view of its role and financial performance. Trinity has, too, been the premier scientific college since the time of Newton – it has had more Nobel Laureates than many countries, including for instance France. These considerations have helped greatly in validating the concept of the science park as a creative mechanism operating at the academic-industry interface. And finally in its Senior Bursar, John Bradfield, the College had precisely the right "champion" for the scheme, who knew his way around the University administration and scientific community as well as the local planning and land development scene. His vision and dedication have been fundamental to orderly and quality development of the Science Park and to realisation of its full benefits to the College, the tenant companies, the University, and the local economy generally.

The Cambridge Science Park now stands, rightly, as the visible and prestigious symbol of the Phenomenon. This is so even though it accommodates only some 10-15% of the high technology companies in the Phenomenon. It has until recently been the only location in Cambridge offering a quality of real estate acceptable to image-conscious firms, whether international or local, and it is still the only site

Dr John Bradfield, a zoologist in the Cavendish who as Senior Bursar of Trinity College has been the champion of the Cambridge Science Park from its inception.

The purpose-built premises on the Science Park of Laser-Scan, the computer graphics firm set up by three Cavendish researchers in 1969.

one can go to and see a concentration of high technology companies accommodated in an increasing variety of modern, and in a few cases exciting, architectural styles. Finally, the Park's enduring contribution has been to help to create the confidence – in the University, in local government and in the local community more widely, as well as in the outside world of industry, finance and central government – that something significant is happening in Cambridge by way of academic-industry links and high technology development.

The story from Holford through Mott to the Science Park and all that it stands for is a fascinating one, worthy of fuller treatment than is possible here. But the story is not over yet. The tensions between, on the one hand, change and expansion and, on the other, preserving the character of Cambridge remain; indeed as will be seen shortly they may have entered a new phase of complexity and controversy.

Take-off

In the mid-late 1970's the pattern of early development just described started intensifying – this was evident from our description straying into the later period. In terms of the formation of new firms, numbers employed, acquisition by large outside firms and a variety of other indicators, the pace and the scale of change in the local high technology sector have accelerated over the past decade. New developments have taken place too: large companies have set up their own specialist operations in the area, the financial and business services sector has grown dramatically in size and sophistication, and the industrial and commercial property market has been exceptionally active, notably including speculative development of several science parks and related schemes.

In terms of sheer numbers the changes are impressive for what is a small local economy (the total catchment area at present has a population of about 250,000, the size of a typical London borough). As already stated, in mid-1987 there were around 450-500 high technology companies in the Cambridge area; around half of these had been set up after 1980. Altogether these firms accounted for some 17,500 jobs, the equivalent of about 13% of employment in the Cambridge area – double the national average for the proportion of high technology jobs in the labour force. Growth of high technology firms has been of the order of 8% a year since the late 1970's, virtually all of it coming from firms set up in the period.

The robustness of this growth was shown by the fact that, despite the gloomy prognostications made at the time, the local economy was barely affected by the severe difficulties encountered in the mid-1980's by Acorn Computers and Sinclair Research, then two of the country's leading microcomputer companies. Acorn had grown to well over 400 people and was unable to cope with the collapse of the personal computer market in 1985. After a fraught period the company was 80% acquired by Olivetti, and a programme of rationalisation successfully embarked on; employment has built up to over 400 again after falling to some 200.

Sinclair Research went through a variety of management changes before being acquired in 1986 by Amstrad. Sinclair, no stranger to the vicissitudes of business, has maintained a Cambridge base and with a small group from his former research team is currently engaged in an ambitious silicon wafer technology development project heavily backed by venture capital and other financial interests.

The burgeoning of high technology and related business in the Cambridge area is distinctive in its qualitative aspects too. In part this is because the leading role continues to be played by start-up and growth of locally formed and independent small firms, most of them engaged in research/design/development of high value, low volume production. In part too it is because of the broad sectoral base – scientific instruments, electronics and telecommunications, computing hardware and software, scientific consultancy and R&D, speciality chemicals and biotechnology – which is one of the reasons why the area has withstood so well the post-1985 decline in the personal computer market.

The qualitative aspects of the Phenomenon are also distinctive because of the nature and calibre of the organisations involved. A list of some of

Dr Hermann Hauser, Cambridge physicist, co-founder with Chris Curry of Acorn Computers in 1978 and now Vice-President (Research) for Olivetti world-wide.

the large technology-based companies recently established in the area illustrates this:

* Schlumberger, the French-American drilling technology group, with strong links with University scientists;
* Napp Laboratories (whose building, like Schlumberger's, has introduced an exciting new element to the otherwise generally conventional industrial architecture) and other pharmaceutical and biotechnology companies including Warner-Lambert (with close links with the University's Pathology Department), various members of the Dutch AKZ0 group, and the Danish-based Novo group (which recently bought out IQ Bio, a 1981 spin-out of the University's Biochemistry Department and which Acorn and its principals had helped establish);
* computer hardware and software companies like Computervision (an internationally leading CAD company which in 1984 acquired Cambridge Interactive Systems (CIS), a spin-out from the Computer-Aided Design Centre, Evans and Sutherland (a world leader in computer graphics which in 1982 had bought out Shape Data, like CIS another successful local CAD firm, that had been started in 1974 by researchers mostly from the University's Computer Laboratory), IBM (now with a listening post on the Science Park), Logica (with establishment of its UK technical centre as the focal point of the company's most advanced research), and Data General and SRI (with small specialist research groups).
* GEC which in 1985 set up an underwater research group through its Marconi subsidiary and in 1987 announced that Cambridge would become one of its main UK research centres;
* Nickerson Seeds (part of the Shell group) and Twyford Seeds, both attracted by the local capability in plant genetics built up over many years at the Plant Breeding Institute and reinforced more recently by formation of the Agricultural Genetics Company.

Partial as it is, this list is testimony to the diversity and quality of recent developments. Growth of the financial and business services sector, partly as a direct consequence of the growth of high technology industry and partly because Cambridge is increasingly seen as a natural business capital for the East Anglia and East Midlands regions, is impressive in its own right too.

Each of the world's big eight accounting and associated management consultancy firms now has a sizeable Cambridge presence. A City of London merchant bank, Singer & Friedlander, has made Cambridge one of its provincial centres. In addition to Prelude Technology Investments, the CCL spin-out mentioned earlier, there are other local sources of venture and business development capital; of these the Cambridge Capital Group has been especially innovative in creating new investment instruments and in mobilising funds from the colleges, City of London institutions and beyond. Among the business support and advisory groups Cambridge Venture Management occupies a distinctive position; its fledgling companies include Tadpole Technology, now

Andy Hopper, lecturer in the University Computer Laboratory involved from early on in Acorn Computers and director of Olivetti's Cambridge research team recently set up by Hermann Hauser.

successfully launched, set up in 1982 by two recent Cambridge graduates.

The industrial and commercial property market has witnessed parallel developments. Numerous financial institutions and real estate developers have started taking a interest in the area, no doubt attracted in part by the cachet of Cambridge but principally by the substantial demand evident in the area. The Trinity College Science Park has played an influential role in this respect too. St John's College has followed suit on a site opposite the Trinity Park, though with a different style and targeted at start-up businesses, especially those with University origins (recent graduates in particular) and with a strong technological dimension.

There are numerous small schemes of refurbishment and in-fill development, most of them contributing to enhancement of the built environment. There are larger schemes too. One of the most interesting is Castle Park, on a previously derelict six-acre site within ten minutes walk of the city centre that belonged to the County Council, which is aimed at R&D and office firms. It seems that there is little difficulty in attracting outside property and financial interests to Cambridge.

This story of all the new things happening on the local high technology and business scene could be continued in different directions, and different people and projects could be named. But arbitary as it is to have named some but not others, enough has now been said to have conveyed the activity and diversity of what goes to make up the Phenomenon and to have stressed the role of individuals no less than established organisations in driving it onwards.

It is in many respects an extraordinary story, all the more so in that it has never been planned or even conceived as a totality. That a leading centre of high technology should emerge in a mediaeval market town, set in a bleak rural environment in a region that only recently started being well served by strategic transport links and that historically has been far from the main centres of industrial development is not something that was foreseen even ten to fifteen years ago.

Why Cambridge?

When a local bank manager was transferred from Liverpool to Cambridge in the mid-1970's he was told that he would be going to something of a rural backwater and that he would be handling college, agricultural and other long-established accounts. And yet many of the ingredients of the Phenomenon were already present:

* decades of investment in research – notably physics, engineering, computing and the bio-sciences – that started to mature into commercial technologies in the period concerned, in ways suited to start-up and young firms;

The UK headquarters of US pharmaceuticals company, Napp Laboratories, is the most distinctive building on the Science Park.

Schlumberger's tent-like structure used for drilling research, a spectacular modern industrial building especially when lit up at night.

* a permissive attitude on the part of the University authorities towards academics getting involved in business;
* similarly a strategic perception of the importance of links with science-based industry and a college-backed science park to help bring about such links;
* a nucleus of such companies already in the area, some of which significantly had recent and direct origins in the University;
* a local backcloth of a small and free-standing town with a lively cultural and social life, where scientists, engineers and other professionals liked to live and in which large firms did not dominate the labour market and small firms and self-employment offered the best means of staying on in the area.

It is worth emphasising again that the origins of the Phenomenon and the factors that have influenced its evolution are multiple. The story as recounted so far contains numerous examples and there is no need to repeat them or to add to them merely for the sake of completeness.

But one further story is worth telling for it helps understanding of how the Phenomenon started acquiring formal shape and outside recognition in the 1970's, as well as how effectively inter-personal networks operate in Cambridge. The story is about formation of the Cambridge Computer Group (now called the Cambridge Technology Association).

The Group's origins lay in a meeting in the Eagle pub in July 1979, called by Matthew Bullock (of Barclay's Bank) and Jack Lang (co-founder of

Topexpress, a scientific and software consultancy with especially strong University connections, and whose brother Charles founded Shape Data). Bullock, a Cambridge history graduate, had become aware of the existence of a number of recently formed computer-related businesses whose founders (like Lang) had spun out of, or were still associated with, the University and other local research establishments. The purpose of the meeting was to bring together individuals and firms of broadly similar origins and at broadly similar stages of business development, with a view to fostering mutually beneficial exchanges and collaboration amongst them.

While the Group had little if any effect on the business performance of its members, its formation had several significant consequences. One was simply to give identity and status to the young technology-based firms, which none could have achieved on its own and which was of material assistance in engaging the attention of the local planning authorities and of the business services community, mostly locally but also in London. These benefits contributed significantly to the attainment, more quickly than otherwise might have happened, of a "critical mass" for self-sustaining growth.

A second consequence was, through Bullock's involvement, to reinforce the interest of Barclay's Bank in supporting start-up and other small technology-based companies, many of whom were naive in business terms. Barclay's evident commitment to promotion of such enterprises and its willingness to finance them encouraged new business formation, engendered confidence elsewhere in the business community that young technology-based firms should be taken seriously and also achieved a better understanding in Barclay's and elsewhere of the special problems encountered at start-up and during the growth of such firms.

A natural corollary to the question "why Cambridge?" is "why not elsewhere?". Important as this latter question is, it is not so easy to

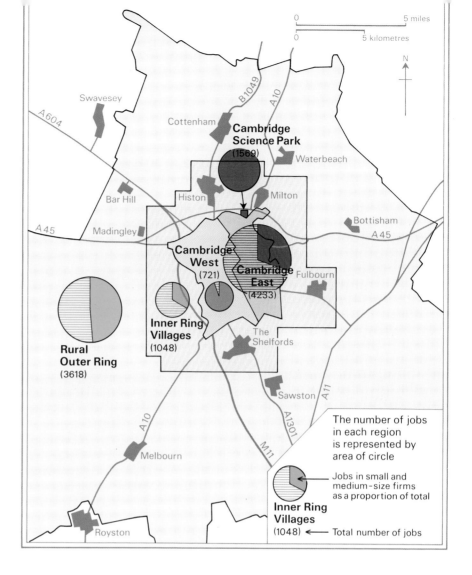

Jobs in high technology industry (mostly small and medium-sized firms) are largely concentrated in Cambridge and its immediate surroundings.

The number of jobs in each region is represented by area of circle

Jobs in small and medium-size firms as a proportion of total

Inner Ring Villages
(1048) ← Total number of jobs

answer. At risk of over-simplification – and avoiding the myriad of factors that go to make one local economy different from another, and correspondingly one university from another – there are two broad reasons to put forward.

One is the consequence of these very differences. The Cambridge Phenomenon is unique, in that the precise circumstances – of industrial history and structure, urban and regional context, research strengths, personalities, University organisation and policy, and so on – that gave rise to and that have shaped the Phenomenon are peculiar only to Cambridge. Other places have other circumstances; and there is no necessary reason why they should work out, if at all, in an economic development process akin to that at Cambridge. That so far there are only two other localities in the world where similar developments are under way – Silicon Valley in California and Route 128 around Boston, both older and on a far larger scale than the Phenomenon – bear testimony to just how seldom this process does occur. But it is worth observing, and consistent with the argument, that "phenomena" of different but not wholly unrelated kinds have occurred in other locations

Harston Mill, reclaimed from dereliction in the 1980's to be the headquarters of Cambridge Interactive Systems, formed in 1977 by four individuals from the Computer-Aided Design Centre.

and other times – in a sense Glasgow had its in the eighteenth century, Manchester and Birmingham in the eighteenth-nineteenth centuries, Prato (in Tuscany) in the 1970's; and so on.

The second factor is that commercial exploitation of a university's know-how can proceed via many different mechanisms. The Cambridge approach, if it can be called that, of new firm formation by academic entrepreneurs is but one of these. In any event it must be remembered that such start-ups account for only about 15% of all the firms in the Phenomenon; the rest are mostly second and successive generations of these spin-outs. The crucial contribution of the University spin-outs has been to "seed" the growth process which, because it took place in geographically clustered fashion, has realised what economists called agglomeration benefits.

At other universities other mechanisms, now invariably on a more deliberate and managed basis, may be used. In an old industrial area, a university's emphasis and special contribution towards economic regeneration may be on transferring know-how to existing firms. This may be done through such means as advanced continuing education for professionals and managers already in employment, special industrial placement schemes for research students and contract R&D and consulting services for small-medium enterprises. Many models of this kind exist – in Britain the Universities of Salford (Manchester), Warwick (Coventry-Birmingham), Strathclyde (Glasgow) and Surrey are among the best known examples – and models of many other kinds could readily be identified.

The Future

The future is both exciting and problematic. The excitement arises out of the exceptional dynamism and special qualities of the Phenomenon which represent economic development of precisely the kind that Britain needs. There is no sign of abatement in the underlying entrepreneurial and business energy. If anything the capability and the potential are becoming greater as the small firms' management experience develops, as the pool of incubator firms for new spin-outs increases, as more large outside firms see benefits in having a presence in the area, as the supply of business and financial services expands and becomes more sophisticated, and as the strategic communications infrastructure and the industrial-commercial property sector continues to grow and improve.

The problems arise, in part, because the Phenomenon still needs to grow if it is to prosper. Given the small size of the local labour market to start with, if it does not grow there will not be a sufficient scale, choice and flexibility in the availability of highly skilled labour and specialised services to ensure that the area remains an attractive location for employers and employee alike.

So the issue becomes one of managing and planning for growth. The concerns of the 1950's-1960's have not been dissipated. Indeed, because of strict physical development controls, especially on the city itself, the consequence in recent years has been a marked increase in parking and related congestion in the centre caused by commuters, shoppers and others. These pressures, to which tourism adds significantly, arise because the Phenomenon has so far been heavily concentrated on Cambridge itself (and a small number of outlying centres) whereas the spatial distribution of where the participants live is more diffuse – increasingly within a twenty mile radius. With few exceptions these villages have no more than the basic facilities by way of shopping and provision of personal services. For these reasons, while the growth in population has taken place outside the City, Cambridge remains the magnet for business, shopping and other purposes.

At the time of writing a new strategic plan for physical development of the Cambridge sub-region (within the framework of the County Structure Plan) is under formulation. How to steer growth of the Phenomenon to locations outside Cambridge – without weakening the very factors that underpin its existence and at the same time alleviating the pressures on Cambridge that could damage those qualities that make Cambridge a special case – is the crucial issue.

There is no assurance that the "right" answers will be found. In the view of a specially formed, *ad hoc* consortium of local interests – from the high technology, professional and academic communities – the local planners are seriously underestimating the already evident consequences of labour and housing shortages as well as the inherent capacity for further

A set of nineteenth century and later buildings at French's Mill near the centre of Cambridge houses several young technology-based firms and others.

business growth. A sense of vision for the future of the sub-region, that properly reflects the spirit and the potential of the local economy and similarly respects and nurtures the special characteristics of Cambridge as a place to live and work, is still badly needed. It is evident that the issues of forty years ago that led to the preparation of the Holford plan for the area have in a strategic sense yet to be effectively addressed.

A second problem of a quite different character arises out of the financial difficulties being experienced by the entire British research system, in which universities in general – and a few universities in particular, of which Cambridge is one – play a prominent role. There is no need to go into all the rights and wrongs of this situation. The fact is that Britain is now the only advanced country in which the resources applied to civil R&D are not increasing; worse, they are declining.

Cambridge is undoubtedly better protected than most other institutions from such reductions and the loss of morale and other negative factors that go with them. But is not totally insulated. And in any international comparison – the only valid indicator – Cambridge research is no longer well resourced. The long-term consequences for Cambridge as a university are clearly profound but beyond the concern of this essay; for the Phenomenon they are simply that in the decades to come there may not be the continuing replenishment of the local research base necessary to keep Cambridge at the forefront of high technology.

Perhaps this is too pessimistic. Perhaps the several new national initiatives currently being taken in the public and private sectors towards the organisation and funding of research will significantly improve the situation in the long term. Perhaps, too, as the Phenomenon grows and matures the University's influence, even as the source of exploitable know-how will become of secondary significance, as indeed has been the pattern in Silicon Valley and Boston.

Whatever the precise outcome, the Phenomenon is clearly at a watershed in its longer-term evolution. It has irrevocably changed the character and supplemented the functions of the city itself – happily in an essentially compatible manner – and its future depends on orderly development of the city and its sub-region as an attractive area to live and work. It will be fascinating to watch how these developments and tensions work themselves out.

Clearly there is nothing automatic about the continuing success of Cambridge as a high technology business location. To a large extent it is up to the participants, individually and collectively, to continue to create the conditions and the opportunities for this to happen.

Opposite: the St John's Innovation Centre, opened in 1987. Walter Herriot, formerly of Barclay's Bank, who assisted the start-up and growth of many young technology-based companies, stands in front.

150

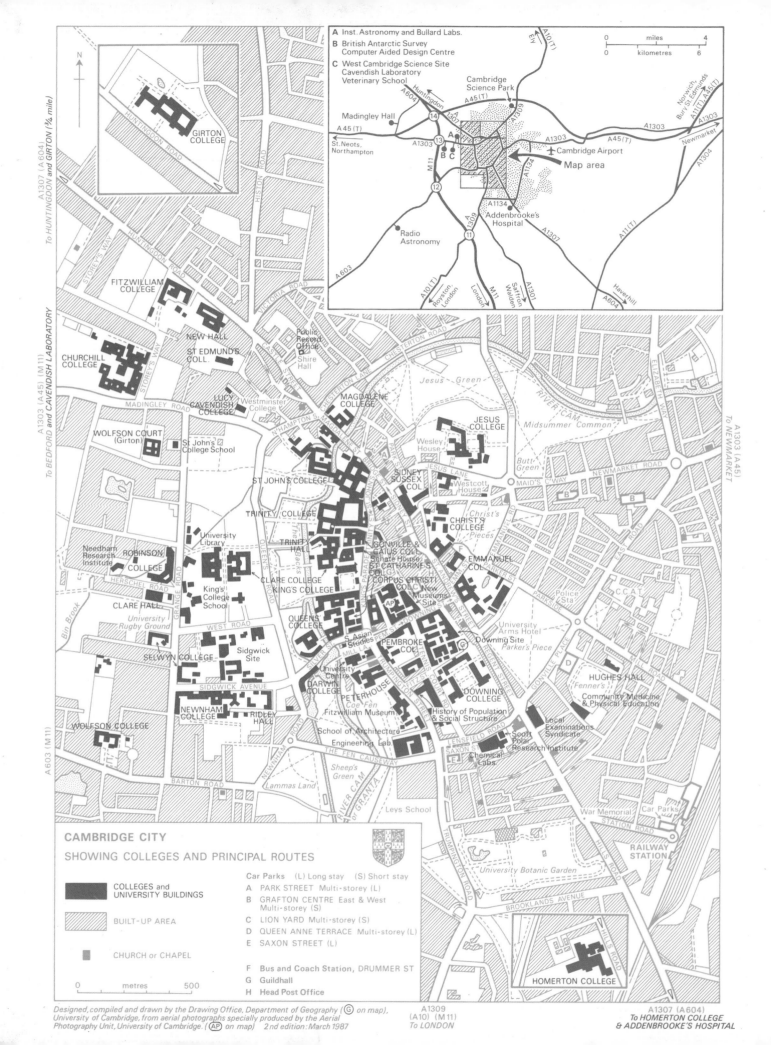

A Inst. Astronomy and Bullard Labs.
B British Antarctic Survey
  Computer Aided Design Centre
C West Cambridge Science Site
  Cavendish Laboratory
  Veterinary School

CAMBRIDGE CITY

SHOWING COLLEGES AND PRINCIPAL ROUTES

◼ COLLEGES and
  UNIVERSITY BUILDINGS

▨ BUILT-UP AREA

▪ CHURCH or CHAPEL

0 metres 500

Car Parks (L) Long stay (S) Short stay
A PARK STREET Multi-storey (L)
B GRAFTON CENTRE East & West
   Multi-storey (S)
C LION YARD Multi-storey (S)
D QUEEN ANNE TERRACE Multi-storey (L)
E SAXON STREET (L)

F Bus and Coach Station, DRUMMER ST
G Guildhall
H Head Post Office

Designed, compiled and drawn by the Drawing Office, Department of Geography (G on map),
University of Cambridge, from aerial photographs specially produced by the Aerial
Photography Unit, University of Cambridge. (AP) on map) 2nd edition: March 1987

A1309
(A10) (M11)
To LONDON

A1307 (A604)
To HOMERTON COLLEGE
& ADDENBROOKE'S HOSPITAL